ISRAEL

The
Founding
of
a Modern
Nation

ISRAEL

The
Founding
of
a Modern
Nation

Maida Silverman

ILLUSTRATED BY Susan Avishai

 Dial Books for Young Readers

NEW YORK

Published by Dial Books for Young Readers
A member of Penguin Putnam Inc.
375 Hudson Street • New York, New York 10014

Text copyright © 1998 by Maida Silverman
Illustrations copyright © 1998 by Susan Avishai
All rights reserved • Designed by Pamela Darcy
Printed in the U.S.A. on acid-free paper
First Edition • 10 9 8 7 6 5 4 3 2 1

Library of Congress Cataloging in Publication Data
Silverman, Maida.
Israel: the founding of a modern nation/by Maida Silverman;
illustrated by Susan Avishai.—1st ed.   p.   cm.
Includes bibliographical references and index.
Summary: Traces the history of the Jews from Biblical
times to the present and describes the events that led to the
establishment of the modern state of Israel.
ISBN 0-8037-2135-8 (trade)
1. Jews—History—Juvenile literature. 2. Zionism—History—Juvenile
literature. 3. Israel—History—Juvenile literature. [1. Jews—History.
2. Israel—History.] I. Avishai, Susan, ill. II. Title.   DS118.S546   1998
956.94'04—dc21   96-6689   CIP   AC

◈ A note about the dates in this book

The abbreviations "B.C.E." (Before the Common Era) and "C.E."
(Common Era) are used by Jewish people and others to describe dates that correspond with the civil calendar. They describe the same dates as the terms "B.C." and "A.D."

Because of differences in the Jewish and civil calendars,
Jewish holidays "wander" among the days—and sometimes
months—of the civil calendar. Israel's Independence Day always falls on the fifth day of the Hebrew month of Iyar in the
Jewish calendar.

To my husband, Marty, whose
unfailing love, support, and comfort
I am blessed to have in my life

—M.S.

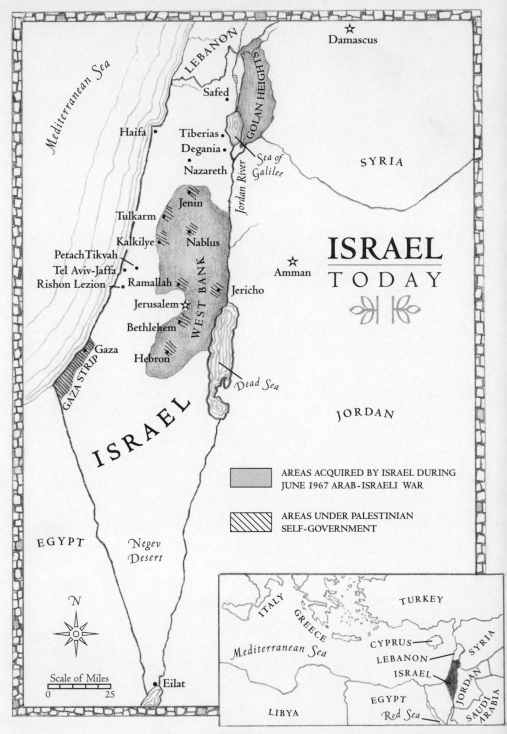

Mediterranean Sea

LEBANON

Damascus ☆

GOLAN HEIGHTS

Safed

Haifa •

Tiberias •
Degania •

Nazareth •

Jordan River

Sea of Galilee

SYRIA

Jenin •

Tulkarm •

Kalkilye •

Nablus •

PetachTikvah •
Tel Aviv-Jaffa •
Rishon Lezion •

Ramallah •

WEST BANK

Jerusalem ☆

Bethlehem •

Gaza •

Hebron •

Jericho •

Amman ☆

ISRAEL
TODAY

GAZA STRIP

ISRAEL

Dead Sea

JORDAN

◼ AREAS ACQUIRED BY ISRAEL DURING
JUNE 1967 ARAB-ISRAELI WAR

▨ AREAS UNDER PALESTINIAN
SELF-GOVERNMENT

EGYPT

Negev
Desert

N

Scale of Miles
0   25

• Eilat

ITALY

GREECE

TURKEY

Mediterranean Sea

CYPRUS

LEBANON

ISRAEL

SYRIA

EGYPT

JORDAN

Red Sea

SAUDI
ARABIA

LIBYA

◼◼ ISRAEL IN THE MIDDLE EAST ◼◼

Contents

❧ Introduction

On May 14, 1948, a new nation was born: Israel. David Ben Gurion, the future prime minister, read a proclamation announcing the establishment of a Jewish state in Palestine. Jews of Israel and the world celebrated with joy and gladness. But Israel was really created on November 29, 1947. On that day the United Nations voted to divide the Middle Eastern land called Palestine into two independent nations—one Arab, one Jewish.

This was an event of great importance. For more than two thousand years the hopes, dreams, and prayers of the Jews had been to return to the land of their heritage. Now the nations of the world had recognized the right of the Jewish people to establish a modern nation in their ancient homeland.

The land is known by many names: Zion, the Kingdom of Israel, and Eretz Israel—the Land of Israel. Long ago conquering nations had driven the Jewish people from their land. Their lives were spent in exile, scattered throughout the nations of the world. But some Jews always managed to remain in the land. And from time to time Jews from the lands of exile managed to return.

The land was fought over and ruled by many nations down through the centuries. Sometimes the Jewish residents of the land lived well and safely under these rulers. Often they did not. But everything would change after that momentous vote in 1947.

One Israeli woman, Margalit, was seven years old when the vote that changed history came through. She remembers it well:

"I had gone to sleep, as on any night," she recalled. *"My parents came and woke me. They looked so happy.*

"Our apartment was in Tel Aviv, and we had a small terrace that overlooked Ben Yehuda Street. It was big—a main street of the city. It was filled with people. I had never seen so many. They were shouting, laughing, dancing, singing, hugging each other.

"The cafés and restaurants were all open. I saw people handing out food and drinks to whoever passed by. I asked my mother what was happening.

" 'The United Nations vote has come through,' she said. 'It was just on the radio. We are independent—we have our own nation! Now Uncle Avraham can come.'

"I stared down at the street. I thought she meant Uncle Avraham was down there and was coming right up.

" 'No,' said Mother. 'He isn't here.' She told me that Uncle Avraham was in Europe and had lived through a terrible war. 'But now Uncle Avraham will be able to come here,' she said. 'He will have a home. And I think he will bring you a present.' "

So many people had spent their lives working to create this Jewish nation. So many had given their lives for it. Now the dream had come true!

Dark and difficult times lay ahead for Israel, but that day in November was celebrated with great joy by the Jews of the new nation. This is the story of how the modern nation of Israel was born.

1
✻ A Covenant With God

The story of the State of Israel begins more than three thousand years ago in a place we now call the Middle East, when a boy gave up worshiping idols made of clay and stone to worship the One God. That boy grew up to become a man named Abraham. Abraham was a wise and holy man, and God chose him to found the Jewish religion.

Abraham's story is told in the Bible, in the Book of Genesis. God told Abraham to bring his family to Canaan, a land that God had chosen for him. Abraham did as God commanded, and God promised Abraham that his descendants would become a great and holy nation. He made a promise to Abraham, saying: "I will give you and your offspring, and their offspring after you, the land of your sojourns—the whole land of Canaan—as an everlasting possession, and I shall be a God to them."

Abraham had two sons, Isaac and Ishmael. God repeated this promise to Abraham's son Isaac, and to Isaac's son Jacob. The promise, called a covenant, was an agreement between God, Abraham, and Abraham's descendants, forever.

One night an angel came to wrestle with Jacob, to test his faith in God. Jacob overcame the angel, who told Jacob that God would give him another name: Israel. This means, "You persevered with God." Israel became the name for the Jewish people: the Israelites.

Jacob married and had twelve sons. His favorite was Joseph. But Joseph's brothers were jealous of the love Jacob had for Joseph. One day they took their young brother, threw him into a pit, and had him sold into slavery in Egypt.

The humble slave Joseph grew up to become a wise and respected advisor to Pharaoh, the Egyptian king.

Famine came to the land of Canaan, and there was no food to eat. Jacob sent his sons to Egypt, where food was plentiful. Joseph met with his brothers and forgave them. He told them to return to Canaan and tell their father that Joseph was alive. His brothers did as Joseph asked.

Jacob came to Egypt with his whole family, and he and Joseph were joyfully reunited. Before Joseph died, he told his brothers that God would remember them and take them back to Canaan, their Promised Land.

Jacob's descendants—the Israelites—remained in Egypt, and their number increased. Many years later a new pharaoh became ruler of Egypt. He feared the Israelites because they were not Egyptians. Pharaoh was afraid the Israelites would join Egypt's enemies and make war. He decided to control them by making them slaves.

The Israelites cried out to God and asked Him to take pity on their sufferings. God heard their prayers and chose a man named Moses, who had been born an Israelite, to lead them out of Egypt and back to the Promised Land. After they left Egypt the Israelites wandered in the desert for forty years before they were able to enter their Promised Land.

During that time something happened that changed them forever. God called Moses up to the top of Mount Sinai and gave him the Ten Commandments: ten important laws that God wanted the Israelites to observe. And He gave His people the Torah—the five Books of the Law that explained how God wanted them to live. This was an event never seen in the world before—a covenant between God and an entire people!

Moses warned the Israelites that someday they would stray from God's laws and be exiled from the Promised Land. But he promised that eventually they would return to it. God told Moses to ascend Mount Nebo, high above

On Mount Nebo, Moses saw the land of Canaan

the Plains of Moab. From there Moses was able to see the Land of Canaan. But he did not go there. Moses died on Mount Nebo. It was Joshua, his faithful helper, who led the Israelites across the Jordan River into Canaan.

The Israelites decided they needed a strong leader to guide them. A prophet named Samuel chose Saul to be Israel's king. Saul was a wise king and a powerful warrior. He ruled the Kingdom of Israel from about 1020 to 1005 B.C.E. (Before the Common Era) and protected the kingdom from people who coveted the land.

After Saul died, David became king of Israel. David founded the city of Jerusalem. He made it the capital of the kingdom and the spiritual center of the people. David was a warrior, as Saul had been. He added to the land. Eventually the Kingdom of Israel stretched from Egypt on the west to the great Euphrates River on the east.

David's son Solomon was Israel's third king. King Solomon built the first Holy Temple, where Jewish people came to pray and make offerings to God, on Mount Zion in Jerusalem. It was a large, beautiful building, made of fine stone and rare wood. The walls were hung with colorful curtains. The vessels used for religious ceremonies were made of gold.

The Holy Temple was the center of religious life and worship for the Jewish people. A special room in the temple, called the Holy of Holies, held a chest called the Ark of the Covenant. In the Ark rested the Tablets of the Ten Commandments that God had given Moses, and the Torah scroll Moses had written from God's word. The Israelites believed that God's divine presence resided there.

Thousands of people came to the Holy Temple from all over the land.

After King Solomon died, his son Rehoboam became king of Israel. He quarreled with his brother Jereboam, who also wanted to rule the land. Jereboam had many followers, and Rehoboam could not keep the kingdom united. It split into two.

Rehoboam became ruler of the Kingdom of Judah, in the south. The tribes of Judah and Benjamin followed him. Jereboam became king of Israel, in the north. The remaining ten tribes of Israel went with him. The kingdoms of Israel and Judah fought with each other for two hundred years.

In 721 B.C.E. the Assyrians conquered the Kingdom of Israel and carried the people into captivity. They never returned to their land. They are called the Ten Lost Tribes of Israel because no one really knows what happened to them.

The Kingdom of Judah lasted longer. During this time prophets—men who brought messages from God and foretold the future—warned that the land would be taken from the Jewish people because they were forsaking God's laws and commandments. Sadly the prophets' words would come true.

2
❧ Destruction

Nebuchadnezzar, the king of Babylon, invaded Judah and laid siege to Jerusalem. No food or supplies could enter the surrounded city. The inhabitants fought bravely, but without food they were unable to hold out against the powerful enemy. In the year 586 B.C.E. Nebuchadnezzar and his armies entered the defeated city. The king killed three hundred of the city's defenders. On the ninth day of the Jewish month of Av, he set fire to the Holy Temple and all the houses in Jerusalem. He destroyed Jerusalem's walls.

A time of great and terrible tragedy began for the Jewish people—the Babylonian Exile. It marked the beginning of the Jewish Diaspora, the dispersion of the Jews among the nations of the world. Nebuchadnezzar carried almost twenty thousand Jews into captivity in Babylon. Their arms and legs wrapped with heavy chains, the Jews were taken from the land of their heritage. A pitiful remnant— the poorest of the poor—were allowed to remain.

The prophet Jeremiah watched in despair as the Jewish captives were led away to exile in Babylon. He tried to comfort them, saying that scattered as they would become, living in other lands, they would someday be gathered together and be given the Land of Israel:

"I will turn your captivity, and gather you from all the nations, and from all the places where I have driven you, said the Lord, and I will bring you back to the place where I caused you to be carried away captive. . . ."

The Jewish captives being taken into exile vowed never to forget the land of their heritage. In the words of the Psalmist:

"If I forget thee, O Jerusalem;
Let my right hand forget her cunning.
Let my tongue cleave to the roof of my mouth,
If I remember thee not;
If I set not Jerusalem
above my chiefest joy."

Jerusalem became a desolate place where wild beasts roamed. Other prophets offered consolation to the grief-stricken people. Isaiah promised that Zion—the name for the Jewish people and their Promised Land—would eventually be reclaimed. God, he said, would always be with them and would return them to their land. The prophet Ezekiel promised that God would take them from the nations where they had gone, bring them into their land, and make them one nation.

Almost fifty years passed. Cyrus, emperor of Persia, now controlled the lands once conquered by the Babylonians. In 538 B.C.E. he permitted the Jewish exiles to return to Judah. Many did so with joy and rebuilt the city of Jerusalem and the Holy Temple.

As the centuries passed, the tiny nation of Judah became surrounded by larger and more powerful nations that wanted to control it. In 331 B.C.E. a Greek general named Alexander the Great conquered the Persians and became ruler of the land. He respected the Jews and permitted them to worship God and govern themselves.

After Alexander died, the lands he had controlled were ruled by Greek kings. They used cruelty and oppression to force the Jews to adopt Greek ways and worship Greek gods. A successful Jewish revolt against Greek tyranny was led by Judah Maccabee. His followers formed their own state in 141 B.C.E. It laster for fewer than a hundred years.

In 63 B.C.E. the Roman emperor Pompey captured Jerusalem for Rome. The Romans called the land Judaea. The Roman Empire was the largest in the world, and the most powerful. Rome's conquered peoples were expected to adopt Roman ways and worship Roman gods. Most of them were glad to do so. They reasoned that if their own gods had been strong and true, the Romans would not have defeated them. The Jews were different. They clung faithfully to God and their religion.

The Romans were harsh rulers. There was great unrest in Judaea, and dissenters were everywhere, calling for revolt against Rome. Pontius Pilate, the Roman governor of Judaea, was particularly worried about a man called Jesus of Nazareth. His followers believed him to be the Messiah—God's liberator. When people began calling Jesus King of the Jews, Pilate feared Jesus might lead a rebellion against Rome. He had Jesus put to death. A man named Paul of Tarsus carried the teachings of Jesus to nearby lands. Paul gained a large following among the people who lived there. His teachings helped to spread a new faith—Christianity.

The Jews of Judaea continued to resist Roman rule. This enraged the Roman ruler. After many years of Jewish defiance the Roman emperor Nero decided to crush these rebellious people once and for all. He sent Vespasian, his greatest general, to Judaea. Vespasian and fifty thousand Roman soldiers laid siege to Jerusalem. The Jews fought fiercely to defend their city. They knew there would be no mercy from the Romans. The battle was a desperate one—victory or death.

In 70 C.E. (Common Era), on the ninth day of the month of Av—always a tragic day in Jewish history—a fire that had been set by Roman soldiers the previous night consumed the Holy Temple. Many Jews leaped into the flames rather than live to see the temple destroyed. Despite this terrible blow Jewish warriors continued to defend Jerusalem. But weakened by many months of fighting and hunger, they could no longer repel the enemy. Jerusalem fell to the Romans.

General Titus, Vespasian's son, ordered the slaughter of hundreds of Jews. Thousands were taken away in chains, to be led in triumph through the streets of Rome, then sold as slaves. Roman soldiers had robbed the Holy Temple before destroying it. The temple's sacred treasures, including the golden seven-branched menorah, were paraded in triumph, along with the Jewish captives.

So befell a second great calamity for the Jewish people—destruction of the Holy Temple and tragic exile from Zion, the Land of their Heritage. The Second Temple, the central place of Jewish spiritual life and worship, was no more. All that was left was part of the western wall.

The Jews were scattered among the nations. But two

Rome's capture of Jerusalem in 70 C.E. led to tragic exile for the Jews

embers, alight among the ashes of destruction, would save the Jewish people. One "ember" was a Jewish princess named Bernice. Titus had fallen in love with her and was willing to grant her wishes. Bernice realized that Jews living elsewhere in the vast Roman empire were in great danger. Roman hatred toward them had been worsened by the long battle for Jerusalem. She begged Titus to make sure their lives were spared. Titus granted her plea. The lives of the Jews in the Diaspora—that great dispersion of Jews into exile when the First Temple was destroyed—were saved.

The other "ember" was a frail, elderly scholar named Rabbi Yochanan ben Zakkai, a follower of Hillel, great sage of the Jewish people. The rabbi lived in Jerusalem. When he realized the city was going to fall, he devised a bold plan to preserve the Jewish religion. Rabbi ben Zakkai told his students to announce that he had died. They did so and received permission to carry his body out of the besieged city for burial.

Once outside the walls, the rabbi made his way to the Roman camp and General Vespasian's tent. The elderly scholar greeted him, calling Vespasian "Emperor." Vespasian replied that he was a general, not an emperor. Rabbi ben Zakkai told him Jewish prophets had foretold that Judah's conqueror would rule the Roman Empire.

The rabbi's words greatly pleased the general. To be emperor of Rome was his secret ambition. Suddenly a Roman soldier rushed into the tent with a message. Emperor Nero had died and the Roman Senate had named Vespasian emperor.

Vespasian was greatly impressed by Rabbi ben Zakkai's vision. He offered to grant him a favor. The rabbi did not want gold or silver. He asked for permission to establish a small place of study for his few remaining students. This seemed a small, unimportant request. Vespasian granted it.

Rabbi ben Zakkai hastened to put his plan into effect. He and his students went to Yavneh, a city east of Jerusalem. When Jerusalem fell, the rabbi and his followers wept and tore their garments. But they could not mourn for long—there was work to be done. The Holy Temple, long the place of Jewish worship, was no more. Judaism must not be allowed to perish along with it.

3 Exile

In the years that followed, Rabbi ben Zakkai's teachings were carried to the Jews dispersed among the nations. The revered sage gave hope to his people, and he and his students preserved the Jewish religion during the long centuries of exile from the land of their heritage.

The final Jewish revolt against Roman rule began in 132 C.E. Hadrian was Rome's emperor. At first he agreed to let Jewish leaders rebuild Jerusalem and the Holy Temple. Jews returned from distant lands to help. But enemies of the Jews convinced Hadrian that such permission would encourage Jewish unrest. Hadrian announced that Jerusalem had to be rebuilt as a Roman city, not a Jewish one. The temple could be rebuilt, but not on its former site. Angered by Hadrian's deceit, the Jews plotted revolt.

The rebellion was led by a man named Simon Bar Kochba. After he and his small army defeated some of Rome's finest soldiers, Hadrian sent Julius Severus, his most powerful general, with orders to destroy them. The Roman general decided to starve the Jews into surrender. Bar Kochba and his soldiers retreated to a city called Bethar. They were joined by refugees from all over the land.

Severus besieged the city for a year. Thanks to underground passageways the people were able to get food. A brook that ran through the city provided water. But the Romans learned of the passageways and stopped food from entering the city. On the ninth of Av in 135 Bar Kochba died. Bethar fell, and Roman soldiers murdered the inhabitants.

Most of Hadrian's soldiers had died putting down the Jewish revolt. The emperor was furious. He decided to take cruel revenge upon the defeated people. Thousands of captured Jews were sold into slavery. Only a handful managed to escape. They fled across the Euphrates River into safety in Arabia.

Hadrian wanted to destroy all Jewish ties to the land of their heritage. He changed the name of Judaea to Syria Palestina—Palestine. The name was taken from the Philistines, ancient enemies of the Jews. Jerusalem was burned to the ground, the earth plowed up. It was later rebuilt as a Roman city and renamed Aelia Capitolina. Jews were forbidden to enter; the penalty for doing so was death. A temple to Roman gods was built where the Holy Temple once stood.

A small remnant of Jews had survived the destruction. The community gradually recovered and grew larger as Jews who had been living in other lands made their way back. Time passed. Palestine was desired by many nations. One ruler conquered the land, only to be replaced by another. But the tiny Jewish community managed to survive.

In 324, a man named Constantine became the first Christian emperor of Rome. He made Christianity the official religion of the Roman Empire. The ancient Jewish homeland became a mostly Christian city. Constantine had churches built at Christian holy places. Christians were free to live in Jerusalem, but the emperor permitted Jews to enter only once a year, on the ninth day of Av, to mourn the destruction of their Holy Temple.

In 610 the Persians invaded Palestine. The Jews of Palestine supported them, and the grateful Persians allowed the Jews to live in Jerusalem and rule themselves. During this time a new religion arose in Arabia, a vast land east of Palestine. An Arab named Mohammed traveled the land, announcing that he was God's messenger. The Arabians accepted Mohammed's teachings. The new religion was called Islam, and its followers Muslims.

Islam spread quickly. In 637 C.E. Muslim Arabs gained control of Syrian Egypt and Palestine. Muslims brought the language and culture of Arabia to the countries they ruled. Within this culture art, music, poetry, and science flourished. Mohammed taught that Muslims were Abraham's children, descended from his son Ishmael. He called Jews the People of the Book. They were protected and welcomed in Palestine. Jews began returning there from other lands, to live and study.

In 1072 Turkish Muslims called Seljuks gained control of Palestine. They treated Jews well, and the Jewish population slowly increased. But as the century drew to an end, Seljuks began destroying Christian churches and attacking Christian pilgrims traveling to Jerusalem. In 1095 Pope Urban II called for a crusade—a holy war—to take Jerusalem from the Arabs. Soldiers from countries in northwest Europe formed a great army and marched on Jerusalem. In 1099, after a five-week siege, they captured the city.

The Crusaders, in their great hatred of people who were not Christian, killed most of the city's Muslims and Jews. They established a kingdom in Palestine but remained a minority in the land. The Crusaders did not rule for very long. In 1187 the Muslims, led by a soldier named Saladin, again regained control. Jews were permitted to return to Jerusalem. At one point three hundred rabbis arrived from England and France. Some went to live in the city of Acre. Others settled in Jerusalem.

The Jews of Palestine fared well under Saladin's rule. Maimonides, a great Jewish sage, was a physician to the royal court of Saladin and was greatly respected by him. Jews were allowed to live and worship as they wished. The Muslims rebuilt Jerusalem, and for a time the Jews prospered in Palestine.

Saladin died in 1193. As the years passed, Muslim rulers began enacting laws that restricted Jewish life. Eventually most Jews were forced to leave the land. By the end of the twelfth century the once-large Jewish community had become very small.

Christian Crusaders returned to Palestine after Saladin's death. In 1291 they were finally defeated by Muslim warriors called Mamluks. They ruled Palestine from Damascus, the capital city of Syria. Palestine suffered greatly under Mamluk rule. Fearful of returning Crusaders, the Mamluks destroyed many ports. Cities fell into ruin. Jerusalem was all but abandoned. The few Jews who managed to remain there lived in desperate poverty. The land was laid waste by sickness, plagues of locusts, and terrible earthquakes. Its inhabitants struggled to survive as best they could.

4
❧ Returning

Rabbi Moshe ben Nachman, a great Jewish sage, traveled from Spain to the Holy Land in 1267. His plan was to study and teach in Jerusalem. But when he arrived in Jerusalem, the rabbi was shocked by what he found. Jerusalem was in a pitiful state. Most of the inhabitants had fled to the countryside. Two Jewish families were all that were left in the entire city.

A group of Jews recently arrived from Europe had brought a Torah scroll with them. They joined the rabbi. Together they built new homes in the rubble of the holy city. In 1306 the Jews of France were expelled from that country. Some came to Jerusalem. Slowly the Jewish population was growing again.

In 1488 a rabbi named Ovadiah of Bartenura left his native Italy to settle in Palestine. The journey took six months. At one point the rabbi's ship was caught in a terrible storm, and he almost drowned. The land journey took him over hot, stifling deserts where bandits and lack of food and water were a constant worry. He described his adventures in letters that he wrote to his family. Rabbi Ovadiah established a school in Jerusalem and taught there for more than forty years.

At the time when Columbus discovered America, the late 1400's, Sephardic Jews—the Jews of Spain and Portugal—suffered cruel persecutions and were forced to flee for their lives. Many of those exiles made their way to Palestine. The new arrivals found only seventy Jewish families living there. The Sephardim came to Palestine without money or possessions. The Jews already residing there were poor too. They did their best to help, but they had little to give.

The Sephardim made up the largest group of *yishuv*, a Hebrew term that refers to the Jewish population living in the land of Israel. The Jews of Europe learned of their plight, and money was sent to support them. It was considered a great kindness to do this, and a way to share the spiritual blessings of those who resided in the Holy Land.

The difficulties they would find in Palestine did not matter to the Sephardim. The long and dangerous journey, the harsh poverty and difficult, unsafe living conditions that awaited them did not stop them. Destruction and rebuilding, banishment and return—these had been endured in Palestine and in every land where Jews had lived during the long centuries of exile. If suffer they must, it might just as well be in the Land of Israel—on holy soil. And if physical life was impoverished, the life of the spirit was joyful. They settled mostly in Safed, a city built among the Galilee hills. By the middle of the century ten thousand Jews lived there.

In 1516 Palestine was conquered by Sultan Selim I, a Muslim Ottoman Turk. His successor, Suleiman the Magnificent, rebuilt the ruined land. Suleiman looked kindly upon the Jews and welcomed those who wanted to return. Several were members of Suleiman's court. Most important was a Portuguese Jew named Joseph Nasi.

Joseph's family lived in the city of Constantinople in Turkey, where the sultan had his palace. Joseph himself was a merchant who knew a great deal about events in Europe. When the sultan learned that Joseph Nasi had contacts in many lands and could provide him with valuable information, Joseph became an important advisor. He enjoyed a special relationship with the sultan. He was concerned about his people, who were being persecuted in other lands. He often discussed their plight with the sultan.

As a reward for Joseph Nasi's faithful service, the sultan presented him with a large tract of land along the Sea of Galilee in Palestine. Suleiman told his advisor that Jews were welcome to come and live there. Many did come— some to the city of Tiberias, which Joseph had rebuilt, and many to Safed. Safed flourished and became known as a city for scholars.

By the end of the 1500's there were eighteen colleges for Jewish studies in Palestine, and twenty-one synagogues. Some of the Jews were descendants of those who had never left the land. Others had come from countries in Europe and North Africa. Most of them lived in Jerusalem. But many families lived in the cities of Safed, Nablus, Gaza, Hebron, and villages in Galilee.

During the early 1600's Jewish life and Jewish religion flourished in Palestine. But the once-powerful Ottoman Empire that had long ruled Palestine began to decline toward the end of the 1600's. In the 1700's the Ottoman Turks' neglect of the country brought it to the point of ruin. Destructive earthquakes and epidemics of diseases caused great misery.

The people who lived in Palestine were burdened by heavy taxes. Large tracts of land were owned by people who lived elsewhere. It was rented, often at high prices, to poor farmers. The beautiful forests of Galilee and the Carmel mountains were cut down. Winter rains swept the empty slopes, carrying away the good soil. In the lowlands the once-fertile farmlands became stony deserts and swamps that bred disease.

A community of Jews managed to survive. Often there were only a few. Sometimes there were many. Their continued presence, like a beacon shining in darkness, showed the way for Jews who made their way back.

5
❧ Changes

Jews had been dispersed into almost every country of the world. Often they were persecuted for their beliefs and endured great suffering. But they never forgot God's promise to eventually gather them from the four corners of the earth and return them to Zion.

Always in their daily prayers, their hearts and minds, their hopes and dreams was the longing: Oh, to return to Zion! An unbreakable chain of devotion, its first links forged in sorrow and despair, forever connected a scattered people to their ancient homeland.

Down through the centuries there were always Jews who returned to the Land of Israel. These brave people made their way back alone or in groups. The journey was long, difficult, and dangerous. Ships sometimes sank, drowning all on board. They were often set upon by pirates who killed the passengers, sold them as slaves, or, if they were lucky, merely robbed them.

Journeys overland were equally perilous. Bandits were a common threat. Food and water were in meager supply. Many people fell ill and died on the way. Those who were fortunate enough to finally arrive in the homeland often found Jews dwelling there in hardship and poverty. The pilgrims and immigrants faced hardship and poverty too. But still they came.

Just as the mid to late 1600's was a time of great hardship for the Jews of Palestine, it was a tragic time for the Jews of Europe too. Jews were not permitted to be citizens in the lands where they dwelled. Always considered an alien people, they were a convenient target, a people to blame when life was difficult. This had been a pattern for centuries.

In the seventeenth century most of the Jews of Europe lived in Poland and Russia. Terrible tragedy overcame them when a massacre of the Jews swept through the lands in 1648. By the time it ended, thousands of Jews had been murdered, their homes and villages destroyed. The Polish and Russian governments did nothing to protect the innocent, defenseless people. Instead, they actually encouraged the violence. More massacres followed.

In 1665 the rise of a false messiah named Shabtai Zevi added to the suffering of the Jews. Thirty years of pain caused a rabbi of that time to cry out in despair: "Is there no end to this bitter exile?" During this tragic time many Jews fled their homes in Eastern Europe and made their way to Palestine.

In the 1700's a saintly man named Israel Baal Shem Tov founded a Jewish religious movement called Hasidism. He believed that God should be worshiped joyfully, with song and dance, and his teachings did much to revive the spirits of Jews who had suffered greatly. He attracted many followers, called Hasidim—Hebrew for "Holy Ones."

The Baal Shem Tov believed that it was important for Jews to dwell in the ancient homeland. In 1764 a large group of his followers left Europe to settle there. Another group arrived a few years later. They settled in the cities of Jerusalem, Safed, and Tiberias in Galilee. The land was still ruled by the Ottoman Empire; the Hasidim rented their homes from Arab landlords.

In the early 1800's Jewish people began calling Palestine by its ancient name, Zion. Zion was the name of a hill in Jerusalem where King David had lived. But the word came to mean more. It described the city of Jerusalem, the entire Jewish people, and the place where Jews would have a nation of their own.

The 1800's began with the promise of a bright future for the Jews who lived in Europe. A new way of thinking had swept Europe in the previous century, a movement called the Enlightenment. Writers and thinkers who founded the movement believed that a modern age was about to be born. Education would lead to new feelings of brotherhood toward all people. Knowledge would replace ignorance. Prejudice and ancient hatreds would disappear.

But European Jews would discover, to their great sadness, that these new ideas for educating people toward tolerance and acceptance for all would do little to change their lives. The new ideas did not end discrimination. They did not lead to Jewish people finding true acceptance in the countries where they lived.

Terrible persecution would bring suffering and death to the Jews of Eastern Europe toward the end of the 1800's. As a result many Jews began to think seriously about settling large groups of European Jews in Palestine. Some did more than just think about this goal; they began working toward it.

6
❧ Grandfathers of a Dream

Moses Hess, a Jewish man born in Germany in 1812, became very interested in the new ideas of the Enlightenment. Moses had been given a traditional Jewish education. But he decided that the Jewish religion had outlived its usefulness. Moses decided that Judaism had no place in the modern world. He believed Jewish people should assimilate—give up their religion—and blend into the ways of life of the countries where they lived.

As Moses grew older, he changed his mind. He observed the continued sufferings of the Jews—how they were discriminated against, even murdered, just because they were Jewish. He suffered discrimination himself. Moses finally had to face a painful fact: Modern ideas and modern education did not sweep away old hatreds.

A man who had set himself apart from Jewish worship and Jewish life, Moses underwent a great transformation. He returned to his people. In 1859 he saw Italy, an ancient nation long broken into pieces, unite. Moses decided the ancient Jewish nation could be reborn too.

The best way to make this happen, he decided, was for groups of devoted people to carry on the work of preserving

Jewish nationhood and religion and someday restore a Jewish homeland in Palestine. In 1862 Moses Hess put his thoughts and ideas into a book called *Rome and Jerusalem.* He died in 1875, and his book was forgotten for many years. But the ideas of Moses Hess did not die. He was one of the first "grandfathers" of a dream: the dream of a Jewish homeland.

Moses Hess had much in common with a man named Judah Alkalai. Judah was born in Sarajevo, Bosnia, in 1799, but he grew up in Jerusalem. He returned to Europe when he was quite young and became rabbi for a town in Yugoslavia.

Rabbi Alkalai lived in Yugoslavia for almost fifty years. He watched three powerful nations—Turkey, Austria, and Serbia—struggle to control the country. He saw the suffering this struggle brought. The rabbi thought about his own people and their long struggles with the suffering that persecution brought. He thought about their longing to return to Zion.

Rabbi Alkalai decided that Jews in Europe should start buying land for a new nation in Palestine. He wanted to form groups of Jews who would go to Palestine and start the work of building a new nation.

Pious Jews believed that someday a messiah would arrive, gather up the exiled Jews, and lead them back to their Promised Land of Israel. Rabbi Alkalai believed this himself. But he decided that Jews ought not wait. They needed to return to the Holy Land on their own. This was a startling opinion, and contrary to centuries of Jewish

Sir Moses Montefiore

Rabbi Judah Alkalai

Rabbi
Zevi Hirsch Kalischer

Moses Hess

Rabbi Abraham Isaac Kook

Five "grandfathers" of the Zionist movement

belief. It created quite a controversy. But Rabbi Alkalai was convinced that a Jewish homeland was the only solution to hatred and prejudice against the Jews.

The rabbi devoted himself to writing booklets and newspaper articles setting forth his ideas. He hoped to make nations of the world understand the need for a Jewish homeland in Palestine. He talked about the importance of collecting money to support settlers. He believed that Hebrew should be spoken in the Jewish homeland. He wanted to see the land farmed by Jewish farmers and defended by Jewish soldiers.

Rabbi Alkalai hoped that England, a powerful nation, would support his plan. He visited there in 1852, to gather support. And he traveled to many other countries, describing his program, urging Jews to return to Eretz Israel—the Land of Israel. He set up societies to help bring pioneers there.

The most important thing, the rabbi said, was to buy large amounts of land so the settlers would have a place to live. He knew many Jews preferred to settle in America, and he was opposed to it. Rabbi Alkalai believed their only true home was Eretz Israel. In his old age Rabbi Alkalai returned to his beloved Jerusalem. He died there in 1878.

Rabbi Zevi Hirsch Kalischer was born in Germany in 1795. He lived during turbulent times. In many nations of Europe people were struggling for freedom and independence. Twenty years before his birth thirteen English colonies in faraway North America had united to form a new country. They had fought a war and gained independence. Six years before he was born, the French had had a revolution, freeing themselves from centuries of oppressive kings.

Rabbi Kalischer believed that the Messiah would arrive after the Jews returned to the Land of Israel. He based his belief upon his interpretation of a phrase in the Talmud, the book of Jewish laws and comments about them. Rabbi Kalischer insisted that if Jews wanted the Messiah to redeem them, they had to do something to make it happen—they had to leave Europe and return to the land of their heritage. The rabbi wrote tirelessly in newspapers and journals, explaining his ideas and plans.

In 1862, when he was sixty-seven years old, the rabbi put his thoughts into a book called *Derishat Tzion—Searching for Zion.* The Jews, he said, had to return to the Land of Israel. They had to follow God's commandments concerning living in the land. This would strengthen and support the Old Yishuv—the Jewish community already living there. This way the yishuv would not have to depend on donations of money sent them from abroad.

Rabbi Kalischer knew that life for the Jewish community in Palestine was often unsafe and insecure. He spoke of the need for Jewish policemen and soldiers to defend the land. He wanted to see schools set up to teach young people to learn how to farm. These efforts would, he said, set the stage for the Messiah to arrive.

The rabbi spent the last ten years of his life traveling throughout Europe, searching for Jews who would put his dream into action. He hoped to go to Palestine himself, but he was unable to do so. Yet Rabbi Kalischer did live to see one ideal dear to his heart come to pass—a school to train farmers was built in Palestine in 1870. He died four years later, in 1874.

Rabbi Abraham Isaac Kook was the fourth "grandfather" of the dream. He was born in Latvia in 1865 and given a traditional religious education. In 1904, when Rabbi Kook was thirty-nine years old, he came to Palestine as rabbi of the city of Jaffa. To be living in the land was joyful for him. But he was aware of the problems there.

Many different kinds of Jews made their homes in Palestine. They did not always get along. Sephardic Jews—descendants of the Jews of Spain and Portugal, and Jews from Arab and Muslim countries who had adopted Sephardic traditions—had different customs from the Ashkenazim—the European Jews who had originally descended from the Jews of Germany. The two groups often quarreled. Many in the Jewish community argued with people who spoke Hebrew as an everyday language. To them Hebrew was holy, to be used only for prayer and the writing of religious books.

Jews who followed traditional Jewish ways were upset and saddened by the new pioneers. Most of them were young men and women who, though Jewish, had little interest in Judaism. Most of them had grown up with scant knowledge of Jewish beliefs and traditions. They were eager to farm the land and build a Jewish nation. But they did not want to follow traditional Jewish rituals and ways of life.

Rabbi Kook was saddened by this. He decided to see what he could do about it. One day the rabbi bought himself a mule. He wasn't quite sure how to ride one, but he bravely mounted it and rode off to visit the young farmers.

Rabbi Kook understood their desire to farm the land as a step toward building a Jewish homeland. But, he explained, Jews who cut themselves off from the roots of their past would have no future. In Rabbi Kook's view God's plan bound the Jewish people to the land of their heritage.

In 1914 the rabbi returned to Europe, hoping to convince traditional, observant Jews to settle in Palestine. World War I stranded Rabbi Kook in Europe. He spent the war years in England. When the war ended, he returned to Palestine.

Rabbi Kook had a great love for all the Jews, even those who did not observe their religion or agree with his ideas. Loved and respected in turn, he was appointed chief rabbi of Jerusalem. Then in 1921 Rabbi Kook was elected chief rabbi of all Palestine.

When Rabbi Kook died in 1935, thousands of Jews lined Jerusalem's streets, mourning the death of this great man. His children saw his dream of a Jewish homeland fulfilled.

In 1845 twelve thousand Jews lived in Palestine, most of them in Jerusalem. The city was overcrowded. But people stayed there because conditions in the rest of the country were very bad. The Ottoman Empire that had controlled the land for more than three hundred years had let Palestine fall into desolation. Palestine's Jewish community fared poorly.

There was no protection against bandits and thieves. Streets were blocked by large puddles of dirty water. Mosquitoes swarmed from them, spreading serious diseases. Food was scarce. Clean water for drinking, bathing, and laundry was hard to find. A few houses had wells. Others had tanks called cisterns. They could store water that fell during the rainy season. But most of the water had to be purchased from Arabs, and it was expensive.

The tall, dignified English gentleman who was visiting Jerusalem in 1866 listened attentively to the words of a young Jewish woman. A new settlement had been built outside the walls of the city. Everyone was happy there— at least during the daytime. At night it was a different story. Dangerous wild animals lived in the lands round about the settlement. When darkness fell, they roamed the streets. No one dared leave home, and no one knew what to do about the animals.

The English gentleman promised help. He went to Jerusalem, found a blacksmith, and asked him to build a large iron cage. When it was finished and brought to the settlement, the English gentleman explained to the settlers that the cage was a trap to catch the wild animals. It seemed like a good idea. But would it work? They decided to try it out. The cage was set in a nearby field and baited with roasted meat.

Next morning the settlers came to see. A large wolf had been lured into the cage and was trapped inside. The English gentleman's idea was a success. The cage trapped all kinds of wild animals. But they were never harmed. The animals were sent to zoos in Europe, which were pleased to have them.

The gentleman who had been so helpful was Sir Moses Montefiore, a wealthy English Jew. He and his wife were frequent travelers to Palestine. Sir Moses was very interested in helping Jews settle the land, and improving conditions for them there.

Much of Sir Moses' great wealth was spent helping the Jewish community in Palestine. He donated money to build homes for poor Jews. He provided funds to educate the children. He built a hospital to care for the sick, a weaving factory to provide jobs and clothing, and a windmill to grind wheat into flour.

Sir Moses made seven trips to Palestine to encourage and support the Jewish settlements there. These journeys were often dangerous because of the disorder and unrest in the Near East. He even traveled to Turkey to confer with the sultan whose government ruled Palestine, to speak on behalf of Palestine's Jews.

Moses Montefiore was the fifth "grandfather" of the dream. He did more to aid the Jews of Palestine than any other person of his time. To honor his generous aid to his people in Europe as well as Palestine, he was knighted by Queen Victoria of England. Sir Moses was loved by his people, honored and respected by Jews and non-Jews alike. He died in 1885 at the age of 101.

7
❧ Hope and Despair

During the 1700's Europe's kings granted greater freedom to their people than ever before. But the Enlightenment had brought little freedom to the Jews. They were still regarded as aliens, not citizens, in the lands where they lived. In some countries Jews were still confined to the walled-off parts of cities, called ghettos, where they had lived for centuries.

Jews were not allowed to own land. Their means of earning a living were few. They lived a life apart, surviving as best they could, guarding the heritage that kept them alive in body and spirit.

Poland had the largest Jewish population in Europe. In 1795, weakened by years of war and unrest, Poland was invaded by Russia, Prussia, and Austria, and divided up among them.

Most of Poland's Jews found themselves the unwanted subjects of the czar of Russia. He crowded them into a tract of land along Russia's western border—a huge ghetto known as the Pale of Settlement. He wanted the Jews kept separate from the rest of Russia. Life was very hard for Jews living in the Pale. The czars permitted them

Life was difficult for Jews living in Russia's Pale of Settlement

few opportunities for work, and they were desperately poor.

Life for Russia's Jews was not very good, but the situation was much better in Germany, Austria, Holland, England, and France. Jews lived wherever they pleased. They could choose their livelihood without any difficulties.

In 1855 Alexander II became czar of Russia. Life improved for Russia's Jews. They were allowed to live outside the Pale of Settlement. The czar's government passed laws allowing Jews to do business in parts of Russia once forbidden them. The dark centuries of suffering and oppression appeared to be over, banished by the bright light of modern ideas.

The spirit of the Enlightenment had spread to many Jews, especially those living in Germany and Russia. Trusting in the power of education and the ideal of brotherhood for all, many of them adapted the ideas into a Jewish Enlightenment. It was called Haskalah, a Hebrew word that means "Enlightenment."

The Jewish Enlightenment was meant to improve Jewish life through education. Up to that time Jews for the most part studied their holy books and learned the traditions and rituals of their religion. Leaders of the Haskalah wanted Jews to learn more: science, mathematics, world history, European languages. And they wanted Jews to learn Hebrew as an everyday language, not only as a holy tongue.

Haskalah leaders were certain that once Jews learned the language and culture of the countries where they lived, they would blend in and be accepted. But if the ideas of the Haskalah brought hope to Judaism, they also brought tragedy. Many Jews who received a "modern" education decided the Jewish religion and way of life was old-fashioned and unimportant, and they abandoned it.

As the century progressed, tragic events in Russia, Germany, and France shocked the believers in Enlightenment. No matter how "modern" a Jew became—no matter how much he or she wanted to abandon Jewish ways and blend into the culture of the country—acceptance was denied. The ancient monster of hatred and prejudice, which they hoped had died, was more alive than ever.

In 1881 Czar Alexander II was killed by a bomb thrown by discontented students. At that time seventy-five percent of the world's Jews lived in Eastern Europe, most of them in Russia, the world's largest empire.

Alexander III became czar of Russia after his father's death. The new czar hated the Jews, whom he saw as an alien people. Several of his close advisors thought as he did. Czar Alexander was a harsh ruler, and all his people suffered. The czar decided to make the Jews into scapegoats for his people's unhappiness.

A terrible time began for the Jews of Russia. The government taught its poverty-stricken farmers to believe a dreadful lie—that Jews were responsible for their sufferings. Pogroms—from a Russian word meaning "destruction"—swept the land. Thousands of Jews were murdered. Jewish houses were burned; entire Jewish villages and districts were destroyed. Police and soldiers did nothing to protect the terrified Jews from rioting farmers.

In despair and panic thousands of surviving Jews fled Russia for other lands. The largest group came to America.

Others went to England. Many turned to their ancient homeland—the Land of Israel.

As in Russia, it became convenient for other European governments to use Jews as scapegoats for the many difficulties that were occurring in Europe at that time. They encouraged their citizens to blame innocent and defenseless Jews for their problems.

Old hatreds toward the Jews were reborn. Anti-Semitism—discrimination and intolerance toward Jews—became an accepted and powerful force. There were riots against Jews in Hungary, Germany, and Austria.

There were even revivals of the ancient "blood libel," the false charge that Jews used the blood of Christian children to prepare matza for Passover. Jewish leaders of the Haskalah realized, to their great sorrow, that hopes of acceptance and equality for their people were in vain.

One of the hopeful, idealistic leaders of the Haskalah was Leo Pinsker, a young Jewish physician. He was born in Russia in 1821. Leo had rejoiced in the promises that modern ideas offered to his people, the Jews.

Then came the terrible pogroms. In Paris, London, and New York there had been angry demonstrations of protest. The pogroms had ended, but for how long? The Jews still suffered. Thousands had been forced from their villages. They wandered homeless, with nowhere to go.

Leo realized that the hopes of the Enlightenment were empty illusions. Jews would never find acceptance in countries that didn't want them.

Leo concluded that Jews needed their own homeland. And he was convinced that Jews had to free themselves rather than wait for others to free them. For a time Leo was not sure the homeland should be in Palestine. Perhaps it ought to be somewhere in North America. Wherever it was to be located, the land had to be productive and offer a sure, safe refuge.

In 1882 Leo wrote a pamphlet titled "Auto-emancipation" ("Freeing Oneself"), outlining his plans and ideas. The pamphlet came to the attention of young Jewish university students who had gotten together in a group called Hovevei Tzion ("Lovers of Zion").

The members of Hovevei Tzion had been shocked by the pogroms in Russia. They wanted to have a Jewish homeland in Palestine. And they wanted Jewish pioneers to go there, farm the land, and prepare it for nationhood. They had even helped form an agricultural school called Mikveh Israel, to teach Jewish pioneers about farming.

The students begged Leo to support their plans. He decided to do all he could to help them and became the leader of Hovevei Tzion. From this group came the first pioneers—twelve men and two women. They called themselves BILU, a name formed from the initials of four words spoken by the biblical prophet Elijah. Translated, the words mean: "House of Jacob, come let us go up"—let us return to our homeland!

These young BILU pioneers were the first ripples that would eventually become a vast wave of immigrants from Europe to Palestine.

8
❦ Pioneers

The first group of BILU pioneers who came to the ancient homeland were part of a mass immigration known as the First Aliyah. The word *aliyah* means "going up" in Hebrew. In synagogues it means going up to the reading desk to read from the Torah scroll. In biblical times it meant going on a pilgrimage to Jerusalem for important Jewish Holy Days. To the BILU *aliyah* meant immigration—going up to the Land of Israel. These young men and women—some only sixteen or seventeen years old—came from cities and towns in Russia to brave the hardships of pioneer life.

Their ideal was to reclaim the homeland that had been taken from their people two thousand years ago. The young pioneers hoped to establish farms and factories, and military groups to defend the land. They were supported and encouraged by Leo Pinsker and the Lovers of Zion.

After a difficult six-month journey the BILU arrived in Palestine in 1882. They found a desolate land. Barren fields, neglected for centuries, stretched away as far as the eye could see. In some places the ground was so stony that it was difficult to see the earth beneath. In other areas vast swamps were home to mosquitoes that carried malaria, a deadly sickness.

Though eager to farm, the BILU knew little about farming. There was only one farm school, Mikveh Israel, to teach them. A farming settlement in Palestine called Petach Tikvah, "Gateway of Hope," had been founded in 1878 by traditional, observant Jews from Jerusalem.

The people who lived there owned and farmed their own plots of land. They shared farm equipment and the profits made from selling farm produce and helped one another when help was needed. Unfortunately a severe outbreak of malaria forced the people who lived there to abandon Petach Tikvah in 1882.

The idealistic young pioneers faced many hardships. Palestine was still ruled by the Ottoman Turks. They made it difficult for the new settlers to buy land. Buildings couldn't be built without special permits. These had to be gotten from Istanbul in distant Turkey. There were few telephones. Mail services were almost nonexistent. The roads were very bad, and travel was difficult and dangerous.

The Turkish government was unfriendly to the Jewish immigrants. But the Arabs who lived there got along fairly well with the new arrivals. The earliest Jewish leaders taught that it was very important for the new arrivals to live peaceably with the Arabs, to respect and cooperate with them.

Arabs and Jews lived together in the same neighborhoods. The children played games together. Jews and Arabs bought food and clothing in each other's shops. As the new Jewish settlements grew prosperous, life improved for everyone who lived in Palestine.

The BILU were soon joined by one hundred Romanian families who were fleeing persecution in Romania. By 1900 twenty agricultural settlements existed, including Rishon le Tzion—"First to Zion," 1882; Nes Tziona—"Zion's Standard," and Gedera—"The Sheep Pen," 1884; and Rechovot—"Broad Acres," 1890. These were in the coastal plain. To the north were Zichron Yaakov—"Jacob's Memorial," and Rosh Pina—"Cornerstone," 1882; and Yesud Hama'alah—"Start the Ascent," 1883.

Hardship and difficulties slowed the development of the land but could not stop it. By purchasing and settling territory in Palestine the pioneers reclaimed and redeemed what they truly believed was the land of their heritage, promised to them and their descendants when God made His covenant with Abraham long ago.

Farming meant more to the pioneers than just providing food. It meant regaining the land. They saw their rough little villages as outposts that would someday help establish the boundaries of a Jewish nation. By 1903 more than twenty thousand Jews had arrived to settle the ancient homeland.

The next wave of immigrants arrived in 1904. These were the Jews of the Second Aliyah. Most came from Russia, fleeing the terrible pogroms of 1903. Other Russian Jews, fearing new persecution after a revolution in 1905, fled also. When the Second Aliyah ended in 1914, forty thousand Jews had come to Palestine.

The pioneers of the Second Aliyah realized that if there

was to be a Jewish homeland, it had to be built by Jewish hands. Until 1904 most of the workers in Jewish settlements were Arabs, because they had farming and building skills the Jewish immigrants lacked. It seemed easier to hire people with such skills than to learn them.

In the eyes of the immigrants of the Second Aliyah, this situation was a bad one. It distanced the Jews from their own land and made them dependent on Arab workers. They were determined to make Palestine's Jews into the builders of a new nation.

The first task was to reclaim the land, and a difficult task that would be. The only land available for sale was the very worst: rocky hills bereft of soil, stone-covered valleys, marshes swarming with mosquitoes.

There was so much to do! The pioneers of the Second Aliyah had no modern equipment to clear and farm the inhospitable land—just old-fashioned tools, field animals such as mules and donkeys, and the strength of their own hands. Living conditions were primitive. Home was often a canvas tent or a makeshift shack.

Men and women worked side by side. They drained the swamps—dangerous work. Most got malaria; many died of it. The survivors labored on. They built roads to move wagons and their few trucks. To halt erosion, they planted thousands of trees on the mountainsides. And as they worked, they sang: "We have come to build the land and be ourselves rebuilt by it!"

The generosity of a man named Baron Edmond de Rothschild was very important to the struggling settlements. The Rothschilds were a famous and wealthy Euro-

Pioneers drained swamps and planted trees to reclaim the land

pean banking family. Edmond's father, James, was one of five brothers who had established banks in the capital cities of Europe. Edmond had grown up in France. His father headed the family's French banks. The family owned vineyards in France where some of the world's finest wines were made.

Baron Rothschild provided money for the purchase of land and farm equipment in Palestine. When the new farmers needed to experiment, to see what kinds of crops to grow and how to grow them, he provided funds. He built homes, schools, hospitals, and synagogues for prayer and Jewish learning. He even helped set up a Palestinian wine industry.

Without the baron's kindness the early settlements could not have survived. He devoted himself, and a great portion of his wealth, to helping the Jewish pioneers in Palestine deal with the hardships and poverty they faced.

In 1910 a small group of pioneer men and women decided to experiment with collective farming. Everyone would have an equal part in running the farm, doing the work, and sharing the benefits.

They built their farm at the south end of the Sea of Galilee, where the Jordan River flows toward the Dead Sea. The farm was called Degania, which means "Cornflower" in Hebrew. The land was purchased from Arab owners with funds provided by an organization called the Jewish National Fund.

Degania's twelve settlers wanted to live simply, share tasks equally, make decisions as a group, support themselves, and share the profits of their labors. They wanted to live in a community of cooperation and friendship, where people cared about the entire group as well as their own families.

They agreed that land, equipment, money, buildings, and animals would be owned by all. A committee of residents would run the community. No one was given a salary. Instead money was given as needed.

Everyone took turns doing different tasks. Men worked in kitchens, women drove farm tractors. The children had their own living quarters, where they ate, slept, and went to school together. They even had their own little farm. Evenings were spent with their parents.

Everyone worked hard to turn barren soil into green farmland. The young pioneers planted cypress and palm trees to provide shade in a hot climate where trees were few. They raised chickens for eggs and meat, planted fruit trees and vegetables, and grew grain to make bread. Cows provided milk, butter, and cheese. The people of Degania transformed the hot, dry, barren soil, yielding green fields with fine harvests. Degania's pioneers suffered many hardships, but they realized their dream.

Degania was the first kibbutz. The word means "communal settlement" in Hebrew. The success of Degania led other pioneers to follow its example. Many "kibbutzniks," as the residents were called, did not practice the rituals of traditional Judaism. But the spirit of Judaism—the body of beliefs as to how people should behave toward each other—was present there.

Pioneer life was difficult, and many had to give up the struggle. But the people of Degania embodied the spirit of the land, and other pioneers would follow their example by founding new kibbutzim. The fruits of the ideals and dreams of these selfless, brave pioneers built the foundations of a Jewish homeland.

Efforts to settle and rebuild the land were carried on by two agencies—the Jewish National Fund and the Palestine Foundation. The Jewish National Fund provided money to buy large tracts of land so that settlements could be built on them. People who could not buy land were given the chance to work the soil and benefit from their work.

The Jewish National Fund also provided land that could be rented for long periods of time for a small fee. This made it possible for people too poor to purchase land to have a share in its development.

The Palestine Foundation helped immigrants make a new life in a new country. It directed many projects and activities in such areas as education, transportation, communication, and sanitation—the many things needed to build a nation and make it succeed.

Both these groups were set up by the World Zionist Organization, itself created by the First Zionist Congress. The congress was founded in 1897 by Theodor Herzl—a great man who would make the dream of a Jewish homeland come true.

9

🌿 "If you will it, it is no dream."
— Theodor Herzl

The Jewish national movement of renewal and rebirth in the ancient homeland of the Jews is called Zionism. It was founded to fulfill the centuries-old desire of the Jewish people to return to the land of their ancestors—the ancient Kingdom of Israel. The idea of Zionism has roots that are strong and deep, but modern Zionism began in 1897, when a man named Theodor Herzl founded the World Zionist Organization.

Theodor was born in Budapest, Hungary, in 1860. At first he seemed an unlikely person to fill such an important place in history. His family was Jewish, but they did not observe Jewish rituals and beliefs. Young Theodor was well educated, but he grew up knowing little of Judaism. When he was still a student, something happened that set the young man's feet firmly on the path he would eventually follow.

When Theodor was eighteen, the family moved to Vienna, Austria. Theodor attended college, studied law, and joined a fraternity. One day his fraternity brothers announced that Jews were no longer welcome to join. However, those who were already members were permitted to stay on. Theodor resigned immediately.

Theodor eventually received a degree to practice law, but his real love was writing. He wrote essays and plays but was best known as a news reporter. In 1891, when he was thirty-one years old, Theodor was sent to Paris as a reporter for a Viennese newspaper. While he was there, he witnessed an event that would change his life forever.

In 1894 Theodor attended the trial of a young Jewish French Army captain named Alfred Dreyfus, who was accused of giving military secrets to Germany. The evidence against him was a document that seemed an obvious forgery.

Captain Dreyfus protested his innocence, but he was found guilty, stripped of his rank, and sentenced to life imprisonment. The Dreyfus Affair divided France and set off anti-Jewish riots and demonstrations against Jews all over the country. Twelve years later, thanks to the efforts of several great men of France, the army officer who had forged the documents confessed. Captain Dreyfus was cleared and released from prison. But his life and career were ruined.

Theodor was deeply affected by the Dreyfus Affair. He was shocked by the anti-Jewish feeling in a country where Jews had lived for many years, and he realized how insecure the Jews of Europe were. They depended upon the goodwill of the countries where they lived. He had seen for himself how dangerously unreliable this was.

The young reporter could not stop thinking about the plight of his people. The lamp on his desk burned late into the night as he put his thoughts into a small book. Theodor wrote of his people's need for a country of their

Theodor Herzl was deeply affected by the anti-Semitism of the Dreyfus Affair

own, where they could be safe and secure. He declared that the task of creating such a nation had to be accomplished by the Jews themselves. He outlined his plan for just such a nation. Theodor called his book *The Jewish State* and published it in 1896.

His plan was not entirely new. He learned of *Rome and Jerusalem*, the book Moses Hess had written. Theodor read it and was amazed by what he found. "Everything that we have tried is already in his book," he exclaimed. But while Hess's book had been all but forgotten, Theodor's little book appeared at the right time. It sparked enormous interest among the Jews of Europe. They looked to him as their leader. He could not refuse.

The very next year Theodor brought together two hundred Jewish leaders from all over the world to discuss the making of a Jewish homeland in Palestine. The group met in Basel, Switzerland, and called themselves the First Zionist Congress.

It was here that Theodor Herzl founded the World Zionist Organization, dedicated to the creation of a lawful Jewish homeland in Palestine that would be recognized by the nations of the world. To help make this happen, Jewish people were asked to join Zionist groups in the countries where they lived. They were asked to contribute money to help buy land from Arab owners and support settlements.

Some Jews proposed a Jewish nation in a place other than Palestine. In 1901 the British government offered land in Uganda, in British East Africa, for a Jewish state. Theodor thought Uganda might be a temporary shelter for Jews fleeing pogroms in Russia. He did not mean it to replace Palestine. But most Zionists believed that because of the powerful Jewish ties to Zion, only Palestine would have the power to inspire the work needed to build a Jewish homeland. Theodor believed so too. The proposal was refused.

Theodor Herzl worked tirelessly as a goodwill ambassador for his people. He realized that cooperation and sympathy from the nations of the world were needed to realize his dream. Theodor met with kings, rulers, government officials. A handsome, dignified man with dark brown hair, a curly brown beard, and a powerful personality, he commanded respect and interest wherever he went.

The path Theodor walked was not a smooth one. There were many Jews who did not accept the plan for a Jewish homeland in Palestine or anywhere else. Very pious Jews believed that, as the Bible said, only the Messiah could lead the Jewish people back to their land. Other Jews thought of Judaism as a religion like any other, not connected to a special place. Still others were afraid that if they supported the Zionists, they would be seen as disloyal to the countries where they lived.

Despite these problems, Theodor struggled on. There was much to do. Though his health was failing, Theodor refused to abandon his work. He continued his travels and meetings, giving hope and encouragement to his people. Theodor was not physically strong. But his heart was filled with the passion to realize the dream of a secure homeland for the Jewish people. He said, "If you will it, it is no dream."

A great rabbi once said that while it was not always possible to complete the work, one must nevertheless begin it. Theodor Herzl did not live to see his dream of a Jewish homeland in Palestine come to pass. He died on July 3, 1904, at the age of forty-four. But his memory inspired others to finish the work he'd begun.

10
A Language, a Song, a Flag

While Theodor Herzl labored to build the movement that would help create a Jewish homeland, a man named Eliezer Ben Yehuda was hard at work in Palestine to help build it in a different way. In 1881 Eliezer and his wife left Lithuania and came to Palestine. Eliezer's dream was to transform the ancient language of the Jewish people, Hebrew, into a daily language for everyone.

Jewish pioneers came to Palestine speaking the languages of the countries they'd left—German, Dutch, Polish, Russian, French, Italian, and others. In Palestine Arabs spoke Arabic. Many Jews spoke it too. Pious Jews conversed in Yiddish. Sephardic Jews spoke Ladino—a form of Spanish spoken by their ancestors five hundred years ago.

Eliezer Ben Yehuda knew it would be impossible to build a homeland if people couldn't understand each other. There had to be a language for everyone. In Europe many Jews had begun to revive Hebrew. Writers used it for stories, poems, books, newspapers.

The Hebrew language was more than three thousand years old. The Jewish Bible was the first book to be written in it. During biblical times Jews spoke Hebrew among themselves. After they were exiled from their land, they spoke the languages of the countries where they lived. Hebrew was special, reserved for prayer and religious study. Reviving the ancient language would be a difficult task.

Eliezer found that observant Jews were outraged at the thought of using the holy language to say things like: "I've got cow droppings on my shoe!" He knew that Hebrew, not used in daily life for thousands of years, would have to be brought up to date. It had no way to describe many aspects of modern life. There were no words for things like *umbrella, bicycle, telegraph*. There was no way to say: "Go and buy a wrench for the plumber."

Eliezer and his wife vowed to speak only Hebrew to each other. They set an example for others to follow: Their home was the first in Palestine where modern Hebrew was spoken. Eliezer's son Itamar was the first Hebrew-speaking child in seventeen hundred years.

Many Jews violently disagreed with Eliezer. But he had devoted followers too. In 1890 Eliezer formed a committee to make the old language live again. It was called Vaad Ha Lashon, "Language Committee." Biblical Hebrew had a vocabulary of only 7,704 words. They were the building blocks for a modern Hebrew language.

The committee members searched ancient books for Hebrew roots and readjusted them to fit modern needs. Modern Hebrew words were created from ancient ones. Words were taken from other languages.

Eliezer decided to write a Hebrew dictionary. He labored long and hard at this difficult job. In the room where Eliezer worked he hung a large sign to remind himself: "The time is short, the task is great." Eventually the dictionary would have seventeen volumes listing more than fifty thousand words.

Eliezer Ben Yehuda's committee helped start schools for the new immigrants. Subjects like arithmetic, science, and geography were taught in Hebrew. There were no Hebrew textbooks, so the teachers wrote them as they went along.

The use of modern Hebrew spread as more and more people began to speak, read, and write it. When Itamar first tried to speak Hebrew to other children, they had made fun of him. Now they spoke Hebrew too.

Thousands of immigrants arrived in the land speaking many different languages. Hebrew became a unifying force that made them into one people.

In 1882 a poet named Napthali Herz Imber was living and working in the farm settlement of Rishon le Tzion. One evening he decided to read his comrades a poem he'd written. He called it "Hatikvah"—"The Hope." A man named Samuel Cohen sat listening:

> *"So long as still within our breasts*
> *The Jewish heart beats true,*
> *So long as still towards the East,*
> *To Zion looks the Jew,*
> *So long our hopes are not yet lost—*
> *Two thousand years we cherished them—*
> *To live in freedom in the Land*
> *of Zion and Jerusalem."*

Samuel was deeply moved by Napthali's words. He decided to set the poem to music. He had come to Palestine from a country called Moldavia. Samuel decided to set Napthali's poem to the melody of a folk song from his native land.

Everyone who heard the song loved it. Soon Jews all over Palestine were singing "Hatikvah." Its popularity even spread to Europe. The song was declared the Zionist anthem at the First Zionist Congress in 1896.

When the Zionists decided that they wanted a flag, a man named David Wolfsohn decided to design one for them. David took two blue stripes from the traditional Jewish prayer shawl, because he believed it was a true flag of the Jewish people. He placed a blue Star of David, the six-pointed star well-known as a Jewish symbol for more than three hundred years, between the blue stripes and set them against a white background. In 1933 the members of the Eighteenth Zionist Congress would adopt David Wolfsohn's design as the flag of the World Zionist Organization and the Jewish people.

A language, a song, and a flag are symbols with great power to unify people. These symbols helped to unite the Jews of Palestine and strengthen them for the struggles that lay ahead.

11
✤ Troubles

By 1900 there were about fifty thousand Jews in Palestine and twenty farm settlements. A few years later a brand-new city called Tel Aviv would rise from the desolate sand dunes at the edge of the Mediterranean Sea. Tel Aviv means "Mount of Spring." It was the first all-Jewish city in the world.

In 1902 Theodor Herzl visited England. He met with important government officials to discuss his hopes for a Jewish homeland in Palestine. Theodor was delighted when Britain's prime minister, Arthur James Balfour, showed genuine interest in his plans.

But the road to the creation of that homeland was beset by obstacles. Theodor did not win international support for a Jewish nation. It would fall to a Russian scientist named Dr. Chaim Weizmann, who lived in England, to take up the work Theodor Herzl had begun.

The outbreak of World War I in 1914 cast a dark shadow over Palestine. It meant the end of the Second Aliyah, because few Jews were able to leave Europe. The Ottoman Empire had allied itself with Germany against Britain and France. Some Zionist leaders hoped Germany would win the war. They hoped a victorious Turkey would look more favorably on the formation of a Jewish state.

Others—including Dr. Weizmann, who had become an important Zionist leader—were sure that Britain would win. They hoped that the British, who had been interested in Zionism for many years, would be willing to support them.

In Palestine there was tension and fear. The Turkish government placed severe restrictions on Jewish daily life. Despite Jewish efforts to cooperate with them the Turks believed the Jews were plotting with their enemies.

The war dragged on, taking a dreadful toll on the Jews of Palestine. There was a terrible fear in the land that the Jewish community, cut off from all outside help, would be destroyed. As the winter of 1917 began, exile and executions at the hands of the Turks had drastically reduced the Jewish population of Palestine. And those whom the Turks spared, famine and disease had taken.

In November 1917 the sounds of gunfire signaled the approach of the British Army. In December 1917 the Army, under the command of General Edmund Allenby, defeated the Turks. His soldiers marched on Jerusalem and captured it. Four hundred years of Turkish rule had ended.

Just six weeks before, the Jews of Palestine and the world had learned of a British document called the Balfour Declaration. It was one of the most important ever written concerning the Holy Land. The Balfour Declaration received its name because it was signed by Arthur James Balfour, now the British foreign secretary.

Foreign Office,
November 2nd, 1917

His Majesty's Government view with favour the establishment in Palestine of a national home for the Jewish people ...'

Dr. Chaim Weizmann (left), *Sir Arthur James Balfour, and part of the Balfour Declaration*

The declaration was written in the form of a letter addressed to a British Jewish statesman named Lord Rothschild (cousin of Baron Edmond de Rothschild) and released in London in November 1917. The document was the result of months of conferences and bargaining with Zionist leaders in England.

Dr. Chaim Weizmann played a most important role. He'd met with Balfour, and they had discussed the need for a Jewish homeland in Palestine. Balfour's sympathy for the Jews of Palestine gained strength during World War I. He and Dr. Weizmann wanted to see Palestine removed from Turkish rule.

Dr. Weizmann was a chemist employed by the British government. During World I he developed a chemical that was invaluable to the manufacture of ammunition and to Britain's war effort. His Majesty, King George V, was deeply grateful to Dr. Weizmann and wished to reward him.

The Zionist leader wanted nothing for himself. But he did want something for his people. Thus was the Balfour Declaration born. It announced that the British government favored "the establishment in Palestine of a national home for the Jewish people" and would do all it could to make it happen.

The Balfour Declaration was greeted with joy by the Jews of Palestine and Jewish people all over the world. Thousands of copies of the declaration were dropped by airplane to Jewish villages and towns in Poland, Austria, and Germany. In Odessa, Russia, thousands of Jews marched in a gigantic parade. They proudly carried banners on which were written "Land and Freedom in the Land of Israel!"

The nations of Europe formed an organization called the League of Nations after World War I ended. These countries wanted to keep peace and solve disputes without going to war again. The League of Nations awarded Britain a charge called a mandate to govern Palestine.

Britain's role, during the time that the mandate lasted, was to prepare Palestine for independence. The plan was to establish a national homeland in Palestine for the Jewish people. Under the terms of the mandate Britain agreed to encourage immigration to Palestine, which had been cut off because of the war.

Hebrew was to be the official language, along with Arabic and English. Jews were permitted to have their own schools, with subjects taught in Hebrew or Yiddish. Arabs had their own schools also, with subjects taught in Arabic. Britain agreed to protect the civil and religious rights of all who lived in Palestine, no matter what their race or religion.

Arabs and Jews had been living in Palestine together for a long time—peacefully, for the most part. Early Zionist leaders considered it vital to reassure the Arabs with deeds, not just words.

Some Arabs wanted peace and cooperation. But others did not. There were Arabs who resented the early Jewish immigrants. Some even attacked farm settlements. Still, when an Arab congress met in 1913, its president had stated that Muslims and Arab Christians had nothing but good feelings toward Jews. He spoke of his hopes that "our

Jewish brothers the world over" would help in the successful creation of Palestine, their common country.

The Balfour Declaration caused little stir among the Arab leaders outside Palestine. But those who lived in Palestine had become uneasy and resentful as more and more Jewish immigrants arrived to settle the land. They sensed these new arrivals were interested in something more than just a place to farm.

Palestine's Arabs reacted to the Balfour Declaration with rage, even though they themselves had little interest in a state of their own at that time. They gave out leaflets calling for mass demonstrations against the Jews of Palestine.

Arab riots broke out against the Jews in 1920, 1921, and 1929. British troops occupying the land did not intervene to stop them. Arab bands attacked Jewish farms and villages and rioted in the cities. Hundreds of Jews were killed.

Jewish residents received little support from the British, who preferred to ignore continuing clashes between Jews and Arabs. When the British could not do this, they supported the Arabs.

When the Jews of Palestine realized that British soldiers stationed there would not protect them, they set up their own defense organization. A Jewish self-defense militia called Haganah, which means "Defense" in Hebrew, was formed to guard Jewish life and property from the violence and destruction of Arab terrorist gangs.

The violence ended for a while but started up again in 1936 and continued on and off for three more years. Most of Palestine's Jews did not retaliate against the Arabs. They had a motto: *Havlaga.* It meant "Self-control." But as the toll of Jewish lives lost and property destroyed grew, the Haganah and another defense group, Irgun, did begin to retaliate.

Despite the continuing Arab violence, Palestine's Jews kept working at their tasks. Isolated kibbutzim were never abandoned, though they were often attacked, resulting in much loss of life. New settlements continued to be built, often in remote places. One group of workers would erect protective watchtowers, barracks, and a stockade. Another group stood guard with guns. They often had to fight off Arab attackers.

The work of reclaiming the land went on. It had to go on. The pioneers worked feverishly, often erecting a settlement in just one day. The astonished Arabs would find a new Jewish settlement where the day before there had been desolate hills. During the troubled years from 1936 to 1939 more than fifty new settlements were built.

From time to time the British government sent officials to look into the reasons for the Arab riots and make recommendations for the governing of Palestine. They suggested limiting Jewish immigration to Palestine.

Many Jews died in the Arab riots of 1936. A British royal commission was sent to investigate the situation. They found that Jewish settlement had brought prosperity to Palestine's Arabs, whose population had also increased. There had been 600,000 in 1920. Now there were 950,000. Yet, they concluded, Arab and Jewish interests were too far apart for their people to live together in peace. The commission recommended that Palestine be partitioned—divided into two separate states. One state would be Arab; the other, Jewish.

The British were dependent upon the oil they bought from Arab nations. They wanted and needed to keep their goodwill. Anxious to please Arab leaders, Britain suggested that most of the land be Arab territory. Only one fifth of Palestine would become the Jewish state. A small part of Palestine would stay under British rule.

The Arabs didn't like the plan. The Jews accepted the idea of partition, but not the details of the plan. Partition would have greatly reduced the amount of land provided for the Jews in the British mandate. It was rejected by both groups.

On May 17, 1939, Britain issued a document called the White Paper. It contained a new plan for Palestine. According to the White Paper, Palestine would become an independent state in which Arabs and Jews shared authority within ten years. It would still be protected by Britain.

The sale of land to Jews was to be greatly cut back. Immigration would be severely limited. Only seventy-five thousand Jews would be allowed to immigrate to Palestine from 1939 to 1944. Afterward Jews would be permitted to settle there only if Britain and the Arab majority agreed to it. The Jews were to be no more than one third of the population—a minority forever in their own homeland.

The Jews of Palestine were stunned. Such a plan would mean the end of Jewish hopes for a national homeland, and it seemed that Britain was going to abandon its promise to help the Jews make a homeland. There was no choice but to protest as strongly as possible.

12
❧ Tragedy

In Germany a man named Adolf Hitler had come to power, casting his evil shadow over all Europe. His particular target was Europe's Jews. His goal was their complete destruction. Hitler considered the Jewish people an "inferior race," not even human.

Thousands of Jews fled to Palestine for refuge. But the British White Paper had severely limited immigration. Even though innocent Jewish lives were in danger, the British set up a blockade, a barrier of ships, to prevent boats carrying immigrants from docking in the harbors.

Launched by Hitler, World War II broke out in Europe on September 1, 1939. War brought new problems to Palestine. The land was now inside a danger zone. Jewish people all over the world feared for the survival of the small country on the eastern shore of the Mediterranean Sea. A place and a people, both precious, were in the gravest peril.

An extraordinary woman named Henrietta Szold foresaw the terrible tragedy that would overtake European Jews. In 1912 she had founded Hadassah, the Woman's

Zionist Organization that greatly alleviated the sickness and suffering of Palestine's Jews and Muslims.

In 1932, when she was 72, Henrietta traveled tirelessly throughout Europe on a mission to save Jewish children from the coming Nazi threat. Henrietta begged parents to part with their children. She cajoled the British into letting them enter Palestine. By 1939 Henrietta Szold and Youth Aliyah, a group she had helped found, had saved almost 200,000 children from Hitler's Nazis by bringing them to Eretz Israel.

By 1941 the armies of Germany and Italy were massed along the deserts on the western side of the Nile River. Their plan was to invade Egypt, push through to Palestine, and capture it from their enemy, the British. Battles were fought back and forth in the deserts of North Africa.

Even as war raged, Dr. Chaim Weizmann and a fellow Zionist leader, David Ben Gurion, worked to build up support for a Jewish homeland. Dr. Weizmann often met with Sir Winston Churchill, the British prime minister. Sir Winston was in favor of setting up a Jewish state once the war was ended.

Meanwhile thousands of European Jews were fleeing persecution at the hands of Hitler's Nazis. In order to save as many as possible the Jews of Palestine defied the British blockade and managed to smuggle men, women, and children into the land. But the British turned thousands back, to certain death.

Despite their difficulties with British rule in Palestine, the Jews gathered their forces to fight with the British against their common enemies—Germany and Italy. Approximately twenty-six thousand young men and women from the Jewish community of Palestine volunteered for national war duty.

The brave volunteers fought side by side with British soldiers. Some perished on the battlefields of Greece, Crete, Italy, North Africa, and elsewhere. Many were heroes, awarded medals for their courage.

The Jews of Palestine helped Britain in other ways. Factory workers produced war materials. Doctors, nurses, and scientists provided assistance. Ordinary people welcomed the war-weary British soldiers who were sent to Palestine on leave. All this help was accepted gratefully.

Hitler had persecuted the Jews of Germany from the time he came to power. As his brutal Nazi troops conquered most of Europe, the Jews of every country under German control were rounded up and taken away. Jews from Germany, Austria, Poland, France, Norway, Denmark, the Netherlands, Yugoslavia, Greece, and the Balkan states of Estonia, Latvia, and Lithuania were arrested. Many were killed right away. The rest were sent to labor camps, where they lived and died in inhuman conditions, or extermination camps, where they were killed outright.

Hitler's Nazis spared no Jews. They took the Jews who lived in countries such as Hungary and Romania, Germany's allies. Nazis murdered most of the Jews who lived in the parts of Russia that they overran.

A few countries resisted giving up their Jewish citizens. Denmark managed to protect and save almost all its Jews. The Italians protected their Jews as long as possible. But the Nazis arrested them in the parts of Italy that Germany controlled. In all these nations righteous gentiles hid thousands of Jews and saved their lives, often at great risk to themselves.

World War II ended in Europe in May 1945. Germany and her allies had been defeated. Hitler committed suicide before he could be captured. But a terrible catastrophe, the worst ever to befall the Jewish people, had overtaken the Jews of Europe. Six million, among them more than one million children, had died horrible deaths at the hands of Hitler and his Nazis, murdered for no reason except that they were Jewish.

The world now learned, to its horror, of the Nazi genocide known as the Holocaust. A small, pitiful remnant of a once vibrant Jewish population was all that survived. Homeless, uprooted, many were broken in body and spirit. They languished, crowded into camps for displaced persons.

For these survivors Palestine was the land of hope. Their only wish was to start a new life there and leave the lands of destruction and death behind. But despite the suffering the survivors of Hitler's atrocities had endured, the British government refused to let them enter Palestine—the one place in the world that welcomed them.

Nevertheless, a trickle of immigration began in June 1945. Men, women, children, even tiny infants, many ill and weakened by the horrors of war, were sneaked out, in greatest secrecy, from the displaced persons camps of Europe to ports where they could board ships for Palestine. By December the trickle had become a flood. From 1945 to 1947 at least seventy-one thousand Jewish Holocaust survivors were smuggled into Palestine.

Thousands of Holocaust survivors arrived in Palestine by boat, following World War II

Conditions were very difficult every step of the way. As the ships neared Palestine's shore, they had to get past British agents who were watching for them. And if they succeeded, danger still awaited. Once ashore, the refugees had to be quickly taken to places where they would be safe from the British, who would send them back to the displaced persons camps if they were found.

Jewish immigrants were arriving from Arab lands too. The Jews who lived in many Arab countries found themselves in great danger as severe and oppressive laws were directed against them. Fearing for their lives, they sought refuge in Palestine. A resolution of the difficulties between Arabs and Jews became an urgent matter.

The rising tide of immigration renewed the stress between Britain and Palestine's Jews as well as Jews and Arabs. During this time a political group called the Labor party was voted into power in Britain. This party had been sympathetic to a Jewish homeland in Palestine. But party leaders didn't follow through as had been hoped. The speeches of Ernest Bevin, Britain's foreign secretary, injected a harsh new tone of anti-Semitism into British policy toward Palestine. He was the leader of his government's policy to prevent the desperate immigrants from entering Palestine. The Jews of Palestine realized that they would have to rely upon themselves to secure their goals.

A Jewish resistance movement was organized to bring homeless refugees into Palestine in open defiance of the British. The battle was hardly an equal one. The small Jewish community seemed no match for the powerful British Navy. But the British were not prepared for the strength and courage of their resistance.

Many were the dramatic episodes and confrontations that took place during this bitter time. In the end the British did not succeed. They were unable to stem the flow of homeless, landless Jews to Palestine. Their attempts to arrange compromises between Arabs and Jews also failed.

In 1947 Britain decided to turn the Palestine problem over to the United Nations, the organization of world nations that had replaced the old League of Nations after World War II. The United Nations studied the matter. In November 1947 the world body was ready to offer its solution: the partition of Palestine.

The United Nations Partition Plan was not quite the same as the one that had been offered by Britain before the war. It called for the establishment of two separate, independent states, one Arab, the other Jewish. Both were given fixed borders. The city of Jaffa on the Mediterranean coast would be an Arab territory. Jerusalem would become an international city.

Palestine's Jews welcomed this solution with joy, even if it was not quite all they had hoped for. Britain was glad to be relieved of its mandate. The United States asked for a few adjustments, but thanks to the support of President Harry S Truman, America wholeheartedly supported the plan. So did the Soviet Union. Without the approval of these two nations, the most powerful in the world at that time, it is unlikely that Israel would ever have been born.

The Arabs were firmly opposed to the Partition Plan. They insisted that all of Palestine become an Arab state and threatened war if it did not.

13
❧ Triumph

The General Assembly of the United Nations set November 29, 1947, as the day on which the voting for partition would take place. In actual fact the land already had everything it needed to become a full-fledged nation. It was a nation in every way but its name.

Jews everywhere in the world waited tensely for the results of the vote. In Palestine Jews sat by their radios as, one by one, the nations of the world decided their fate. Egypt said no. France, yes. The Soviet Union, yes. The United States, yes . . .

On November 30, at one o'clock in the morning Jerusalem time, the world was told of the birth of the Jewish state. Thirty-three nations voted for the partition; six voted against it. Britain abstained. When the voting was over, the United Nations, by a majority of two thirds of its members, had voted in favor of partitioning Palestine.

The dream that had resided for so many centuries in the hearts and minds of the Jewish exiles, the hope of the founders of Zionism and the land's settlers and pioneers was about to be realized for everyone, both within Israel and without, who had fought long and hard for this day. A modern independent state, a land of freedom and refuge for the Jews of the world, was about to be born.

On November 30 the partition of Palestine was rejected by the Arab states, who refused the Jews their small, eight-thousand-square-mile homeland. Arab leaders called for a strike of Arab workers throughout the land.

Anti-Jewish riots broke out in Palestine as Arab leaders called for death to the Jews. Mobs of Palestinian Arabs attacked Jerusalem's Jewish Quarter. The British, who were supposed to keep peace and order, did nothing to stop them.

The violence spread. Volunteers from nearby Arab countries joined the Palestinian Arabs in attacking the Jews to prevent a Jewish nation from coming into being. After many difficult battles the Jewish defense groups gained control of all the land that been allotted for a Jewish state.

In December 1947 Britain announced that it was giving up its mandate and would leave Palestine on May 15, 1948. At 4:00 P.M. on May 14, 1948, hours before the British mandate was to end, David Ben Gurion stepped in front of a radio microphone in the auditorium of the Tel Aviv Museum.

Standing in front of a picture of Theodor Herzl, which was flanked by the blue-and-white flag, David Ben Gurion read the Declaration of Israel's Independence, announcing the birth of the Jewish nation.

In it he asked the Arab residents of the newborn nation "to return to the ways of peace and play their part in the development of the State, with full and equal citizenship

David Ben Gurion announced the birth of the Jewish nation: Israel

and due representation in all its bodies and institutions—provisional or permanent." Everyone in the packed auditorium began to sing "Hatikvah." The hope had been realized at last.

The ceremony had been planned to end before the start of the Jewish Sabbath. Now the new Israelis poured into the streets from homes and offices, restaurants, stores, and schools. Cars and buses came to a halt. The passengers jumped out. Joy was written on every face. People laughed and cried. They danced and sang most of the night.

News of this momentous declaration sped around the world. But there was fear along with the joy. The armies of five Arab nations had been massing along the borders of the newborn State of Israel. There were already hostile Arabs living within. The Jews of Palestine were only 650,000 people, surrounded by millions of Arabs.

The first act of the government of Israel had been its declaration of independence. Its second act was to abolish the British document that would have kept Jews a minority forever in their land. Shortly after Ben Gurion's declaration President Truman, speaking for the United States of America, announced his country's acceptance of Israel as a nation. The Jews of Israel and the world rejoiced.

At midnight on May 14 the last British governor of Palestine, Sir Alan Cunningham, withdrew, taking all remaining British forces with him. The newborn nation had little time to celebrate. Less than twenty-four hours later the armies of Israel's Arab neighbors—Egypt, Syria, Lebanon, Transjordan, and Iraq—invaded. Now Israel had to fight for its very survival. The War of Independence had begun.

For more than fifteen months the small nation, poorly equipped for warfare, fought a fierce battle. It struggled against great odds. Its defense forces were not professional soldiers. They were people's armies. The war was fought with one thought in mind—survival.

Every victory over Israel's foes seemed miraculous. What fueled the victories was the Jews' fierce determination to survive, to be free people in their own land, to provide a home for any Jew in the world who needed or wanted one.

The Arabs had hoped to make a lightning attack that would cause a quick collapse of the new nation. But that plan fell through when Jerusalem held out against thousands of Arab soldiers. Only the Old City of Jerusalem, the part of the city enclosed within its walls, fell.

Israeli soldiers launched raids into Syria and Transjordan. Israeli planes dropped bombs on Cairo, Egypt; Damascus, Syria; and Amman, Transjordan. The Israelis had few planes. As soon as one returned from a mission, it was refueled and sent back into the sky.

Degania found itself in the forefront of battle. The kibbutz was on the shores of the Sea of Galilee, close to the Syrian border. The farmers of Degania prevented the Syrian Army from entering Israel, fighting them off with great courage, although they were greatly outnumbered.

Israel's forces finally pushed back the invading armies. But the price for triumph was high. More than six thousand Israeli men and women died defending their country.

The triumph of the small new nation against such great odds made other people wonder if the Israelis had a secret weapon. When asked, the Israelis replied: "Yes, we did. It was called 'no choice.' " On July 18, 1948, a truce was accepted by Israelis and Arabs. By then Israel controlled some of the land that partition had granted to the Arabs.

The truce was often broken. Arab forces attacked Israel again and again. Israel fought many major battles. They won them all. Finally the United Nations appointed a mediator to arrange an end to the hostilities. Dr. Ralph Bunche of the United States succeeded in bringing the fighting to an official end in January 1949. By July 1949 the War of Independence was over.

14
🌿 Israel Reborn

The gates of Israel had opened wide, ready to gather in any Jews who wanted to come. The first to arrive entered Israel only a few hours after the British departed. In the early hours of May 15, 1948, a small ship carrying refugees from World War II entered Haifa harbor. They were greeted with joy.

Great waves of immigrants poured into Israel. Many were refugees who had spent long, weary months in displaced persons camps on the British-controlled island of Cyprus because Britain would not let them enter Palestine. Thousands of Jews who had been waiting in displaced persons camps in Austria and Germany arrived also. They were brought by Israel's own ships and planes.

The gathering in of the exiles, so long a dream, had begun. Jews arrived from everywhere. Russia permitted Jewish war survivors to go to Israel. Jews came from Soviet Russia, Poland, Czechoslovakia, Yugoslavia, Romania, Bulgaria. Jews came to Israel from North Africa and Asia. Many, like the Jews of Libya, Iraq, and Yemen, came because their lives were in danger in the lands where they had lived.

After Israel's creation, immigrants arrived from all over the world

But not all immigrants came seeking refuge. Many Jews came to help build the new Jewish state. By 1951 almost 650,000 Jews had come—more than had entered during the thirty years of the British mandate. Now Israel had to build the nation it had fought so long and hard to regain.

Many difficult tasks and challenges awaited. The new immigrants had to be cared for. Most of them had come with nothing. The Israeli government had to provide homes, food, and clothing. The immigrants had to learn skills that would enable them to be employed and to lead useful, happy lives.

A new government had to be set up—immediately. The government of Israel had to run a police force, hospitals and health care, schools and colleges. They had to establish a money system, post offices, banks, courts of law, and communication systems such as radio and telephones. They had to provide gas and electricity. And the new nation had to establish relationships with other nations.

The strains caused by war and development required sacrifice within. Food was scarce and had to be rationed. Aid was needed from abroad. The American government provided bank loans. The German government gave war reparation funds. Jews and Jewish organizations in other lands raised money and sent it to Israel. Despite the difficulties and hardships the new nation made rapid progress.

The Israeli government used the aid to build houses. They used it to modernize old farms and build new ones. They built roads and factories. They set up a national airline and a fleet of ships for import and export.

Israel held its first election on January 25, 1949. The

voters elected 120 people to its new government, called the Knesset, or parliament. The turnout was tremendous—almost eighty-five percent of all those eligible to vote did so.

Two people who had been tireless in their efforts to bring Israel into being were elected to lead it. The Knesset elected Dr. Chaim Weizmann as president. David Ben Gurion was chosen as prime minister. On May 11, 1949, Israel joined the United Nations. The blue-and-white Israeli flag hung among the flags of member nations on United Nations Plaza, proud emblem of the Jewish nation—Israel.

"My uncle Avraham did come," Margalit recalled. "Many years later I learned that he had lost his wife and child in the Holocaust. After the war ended, he went to a camp for homeless people. Eventually he made his way to Italy and waited there for more than a year, hoping to come to Israel.

"When Uncle Avraham arrived at our house, he and my mother hugged each other and cried. He was her younger brother, and she had not seen him for almost fifteen years. And he brought me a doll. We have it still."

Important Events in Israel's History
1948—PRESENT

1948

- Proclamation on the Rise of the State of Israel: David Ben Gurion announces the creation of an independent Jewish state in territory established by the United Nations Partition Plan.

- Following Israel's declaration of independence the armies of Egypt, Syria, Lebanon, Transjordan, and Iraq invade Israel. This is the start of Israel's War of Independence, also known as the first Arab-Israeli war.

- Mass immigration of Jews from European and Arab countries begins.

1949

- Israel holds its first national elections. Dr. Chaim Weizmann becomes president; David Ben Gurion is elected prime minister.

- The United Nations admits Israel as its fifty-ninth member.

- The Israeli parliament, called the Knesset, passes the Compulsory Education Law, requiring all children to attend school from age five until age fifteen.

- A cease-fire is arranged in the War of Independence. Israel signs armistice agreements with Egypt, Lebanon, Transjordan, and Syria. Iraq refuses to sign.

◄ Hebrew University-Hadassah Medical School, Israel's first medical school, opens in Jerusalem, with fifty students.

◄ Operation Magic Carpet: An Israeli airlift flies almost fifty thousand Yemenite Jews to Israel.

1950

◄ Israel's government passes the Law of Return: All Jews, regardless of nationality, can immigrate to Israel and become immediate citizens.

1951

◄ Operation Ali Baba: An Israeli airlift flies more than 124,000 Iraqi Jews to Israel.

1953

◄ The Yad Vashem, Israel's memorial to the six million Jews who perished in the Holocaust, is established overlooking the Jerusalem forest.

◄ Israel passes the Land Acquisition Law, offering payment for property taken from Arab citizens of Israel who lived there between May 4, 1949, and April 1, 1952.

1956

◄ Egypt nationalizes the Suez Canal, angering France and Britain, partial owners of the canal. Previously Egypt had closed the Suez Canal and the Straits of Tiran to Israel-bound and Israeli ships and had launched a number of terrorist attacks against Israeli citizens. Israel now joins France and Britain in planning a joint military attack against Egypt. Israel seizes the Gaza Strip and Sinai Peninsula from Egypt.

1962

⮞ Adolf Eichmann, a top German Nazi official responsible for the deaths of thousands of Jews during the Holocaust, is executed after a trial.

1963

⮞ Prime Minister David Ben Gurion resigns. He is replaced by Levi Eshkol.

1964

⮞ Creation of the Palestine Liberation Organization (PLO): During the first Arab summit meeting in Egypt, leaders of thirteen Arab nations agree to take a more active role in the "liberation of Palestine."

⮞ After eleven years of construction the National Water Carrier is completed. This pipeline brings water from north and central Israel to the semi-arid south.

1966

⮞ Israeli author S. Y. Agnon is awarded the Nobel prize for literature.

1967

⮞ Six-Day War: Responding to the massing of Egyptian and Syrian armies along the border, Israel makes a preemptive attack against Egypt's Air Force. In six days Israel defeats Egyptian, Syrian, and Jordanian forces, gaining Sinai, the Gaza Strip, the Golan Heights, and the West Bank. Jerusalem is reunited.

⮞ The United Nations effects a cease-fire.

⮞ In the aftermath of the Six-Day War the Arab states pass a resolution voting no to recognizing Israel's existence, no to negotiation with Israel, and no to peace with Israel.

1969

◈ War of Attrition: Egypt's President Gamal Abdel Nasser breaks the cease-fire agreement and begins continuous military attacks on Israeli territory against Israeli military installations and civilians.

◈ Golda Meir becomes prime minister of Israel.

1972

◈ Eleven Israeli athletes are murdered at the Olympic Games in Munich, Germany, by PLO terrorists.

1973

◈ Yom Kippur War: Egypt and Syria attack Israel on Judaism's holiest holiday. Taken by surprise, Israel takes three weeks to organize, counterattack, and halt the enemy advance. Two thousand Israeli soldiers die in battle.

1975

◈ Israel becomes an associate member of the European Common Market.

◈ The United Nations General Assembly passes a resolution sponsored by a Soviet-Third World-Arab bloc naming Zionism "a form of racism and racial discrimination."

1976

◈ Prime Minister Yitzhak Rabin orders a raid that results in the rescue of over a hundred hostages, most of them Israeli, who had been hijacked and were being held by Palestinian terrorists at the airport at Entebbe, Uganda.

1977

◈ Menachem Begin becomes prime minister of Israel.

ᛃ Egyptian President Anwar Sadat arrives in Jerusalem, the first Arab leader to visit Israel. This is the beginning of peace negotiations between Egypt and Israel.

1978

ᛃ Camp David Accords: After twelve days of meetings at the American presidential retreat, Egypt and Israel sign the Framework for Peace in the Middle East.

ᛃ Menachem Begin and Anwar Sadat share the Nobel peace prize.

1979

ᛃ Egyptian-Israeli Peace Treaty is signed in Washington, D.C. Ending thirty years of hostility between the two nations, it is the first peace treaty between Israel and an Arab state.

1981

ᛃ Egyptain President Anwar Sadat is assassinated during a military parade in Cairo by Islamic militants opposed to the Egyptian-Israeli Peace Treaty.

ᛃ Israel annexes the Golan Heights, making it officially Israeli territory, subject to Israeli laws.

1982

ᛃ Israel withdraws from its remaining positions in the Sinai Peninsula in accordance with provisions of the Egyptian-Israeli Peace Treaty.

ᛃ Operation Peace for Galilee: Israel invades Lebanon in an effort to destroy PLO strongholds and halt terrorist and rocket attacks on northern Israel.

ᛃ The PLO agrees to withdraw its guerrillas from Beirut, Lebanon.

1983

✦ Prime Minister Menachem Begin resigns.

1985

✦ Operation Moses, a secret emergency rescue mission, brings over eight thousand Ethiopian Jews to Israel.

1987

✦ Intifada, the Palestinian Arab uprising, begins in the West Bank and the Gaza Strip. Palestinian Arabs throw rocks and use work stoppages and violence to protest Israeli control of the territories.

1988

✦ PLO Chairman Yasir Arafat renounces terrorism and recognizes the existence of the State of Israel at a special United Nations session in Geneva, Switzerland.

✦ Israel launches its first space satellite, *Ofek 1.*

1989

✦ The collapse of the Soviet Union enables its Jews to emigrate to Israel.

1991

✦ A historic peace conference in Madrid, Spain, marks the first time Arabs and Israelis sit at the same table for direct discussions.

✦ The United Nations repeals the "Zionism is racism" resolution. The Soviet Union and the formerly Communist East European nations that had voted for the original resolution vote to repeal it. The Arab countries do not vote.

✦ Operation Solomon is launched to rescue Ethiopia's remaining Jews. Within twenty-four hours almost all are flown to Israel.

⮒ Iraq sends Soviet-made SCUD missiles into Israel during the Persian Gulf War.

1992

⮒ Yitzhak Rabin is elected prime minister.

1993

⮒ Israeli-Palestinian Declaration of Principles, "Oslo I," is signed on the White House lawn in Washington, D.C. Israel and the PLO recognize each other's political and lawful rights, agree to end years of conflict, and pledge to work for coexistence, peace, and security. The declaration includes a plan for provisional Palestinian self-rule in the Gaza Strip and Jericho, followed by negotiations for further agreements and a permanent arrangement.

⮒ Jewish arrivals from former Soviet Union, begun in 1989, now number more than 470,000.

⮒ Israel and the Vatican, the Pope's headquarters in Rome, officially establish diplomatic relations. The agreement calls for fighting anti-Semitism, racism, and religious intolerance.

1994

⮒ An Israeli extremist fires on Muslims worshiping at a mosque in Hebron. Twenty-nine people are killed, many more wounded. Israeli leaders condemn the attack.

⮒ Jordan, Syria, and Lebanon halt negotiations with Israel. The PLO temporarily halts talks with Israel.

⮒ Israel withdraws from Jericho and Gaza. Civil authority is given to PLO-appointed Palestinians.

⮒ Prime Minister Yitzhak Rabin, Foreign Minister Shimon Peres, and PLO Chairman Yasir Arafat are awarded the Nobel peace prize for their efforts to create peace in the Middle East.

⮒ Israel signs a peace treaty with Jordan.

◈| A wave of terrorist suicide bombings begins, launched by extremist members of the Muslim organizations Hamas and Islamic Jihad protesting the peace process.

1995

◈| "Oslo II" agreement signed by Prime Minister Rabin and PLO Chairman Arafat. It details Israeli troop deployment from seven Palestinian cities in the West Bank and elections for a Palestinian council. The PLO agrees to abolish its covenant clauses that call for Israel's destruction.

◈| Prime Minister Rabin is assassinated by a young Israeli extremist opposed to the peace process. Foreign Minister Shimon Peres becomes acting prime minister.

◈| Israel withdraws its military forces from six major Palestinian cities on the West Bank. Control is given to the new Palestinian police force, ending twenty-eight years of Israeli occupation.

1996

◈| Four terrorist suicide bus bombings kill sixty-eight Israelis.

◈| Benjamin Netanyahu is elected prime minister.

◈| Following Israel's decision to open a second entrance to a tunnel running along the Western Wall, Palestinians begin rioting. Israelis and Palestinians die in the clashes.

◈| Prime Minster Netanyahu, PLO President Arafat, and King Hussein of Jordan meet with United States President Bill Clinton in Washington to continue the peace process.

1997

◈| The Hebron Accord, turning over four fifths of this Biblical city on Israel's West Bank to Palestinian control, is signed by Israeli and Palestinian officials. The remaining one fifth, where Jewish residents live, is kept under Israeli control.

Afterword

I grew up with a great love for my Jewish heritage and traditions. But it took a trip to Israel some years ago to spark the special appreciation that eventually led me to write books for children that tell about our heritage.

I visited deserts where the prophets of our people once wandered. I saw tents where Bedouin Muslims live. I thought: Our ancestors probably lived in tents like these more than three thousand years ago. I visited the tombs of our matriarch, Sarah, and our patriarch, Abraham. I dipped my hands in the same Jordan River the Israelites crossed when they entered the land of their heritage. I ate grapes, dates, and figs that came from trees planted by Zionist pioneers who rebuilt this nation. The ancient Israelites had grown them too, when they farmed the land. I'd eaten the same fruits in America, but they tasted sweeter here.

My most treasured memories of Israel are of my visits to the ancient Kotel, or Wall, in Jerusalem. It is all that remains of the Holy Temple, destroyed by the Romans almost two thousand years ago. The vast courtyard in front of the Kotel is usually filled with men and women, young and old. Jewish people from all over the world come there to pray. And high above, among niches in the stones, beautiful white pigeons silently keep watch.

The day before I left Israel, I visited the Kotel one last time. I saw people putting scraps of paper into cracks between the ancient stones. I asked what the papers were, and was told that hopes and prayers were written on them. Because the Wall is so holy a place, people believe the messages have a special pathway to God. They remain until they crumble to dust, for none are ever removed. Some messages must surely have contained prayers for peace in the land. Mine did. I hope our prayers will soon be answered.

—Maida Silverman

Bibliography

Allon, Yigal. *Shield of David: The Story of Israel's Armed Forces.* New York: Random House, 1970.

Eban, Abba. *My Country: The Story of Modern Israel.* New York: Random House, 1972.

Encyclopedia Judaica. New York: The Macmillan Co., 1972.

Forst, Siegmund (compiler). *If I Forget Thee, O Jerusalem: The History of the Old Yishuv.* New York: Schulsinger Brothers, 1978.

Gerlitz, Menachem. *Return to the Heavenly City.* New York: CIS Publishers, 1991.

Johnston, Paul. *A History of the Jews.* New York: Harper Perennial, 1988.

Library of Nations: Israel. New York: Time-Life Books, 1986.

Nyrop, Richard (editor). *Israel, a Country Study.* Washington, D.C.: The American University, Foreign Affairs Studies, 1979.

Rubenstein, Aryeh. *The Return to Zion,* Popular History of Jewish Civilization. New York: Leon Amiel Publishers Co., 1974.

Scherman, Rabbi Nosson (and editors). *The Chumash (The Five Books of the Torah), The Stone Edition.* New York: Mesorah Publications, 1993.

Schulman, Abraham. *Coming Home to Zion: A Pictorial History of Pre-Israel Palestine.* New York: Doubleday & Co., 1979.

Schwartz, Leo W. (editor). *Great Ages and Ideas of the Jewish People.* New York: Modern Library, 1956.

Shulman, Yaakov Dovid (translator). *Pathway to Jerusalem: The Travel Letters of Rabbi Ovadiah of Bartenura.* New York: CIS Publishers, 1992.

Tanakh, The Holy Scriptures. Philadelphia: Jewish Publication Society, 1952.

Zuckerbrot, B., and J. Ditchek. *Lesson Plans on Israel and the Arab-Israel Conflict for Secondary School Social Studies Classes.* New York: Anti-Defamation League, 1992.

Recommended Books for Further Reading

Adler, David. *A Picture Book of Israel.* New York: Holiday House, 1984. A good introduction for the young reader.

Bamberger, David. *A Young Person's History of Israel.* New York: Behrman House, 1994. Informative, focused text with emphasis on the founding and history of modern Israel and its personalities.

Burstein, Chaya. *A Kid's Catalog of Israel.* New York: Jewish Publication Society, 1988. Lively writing and illustrations. Includes history, stories, and culture, plus crafts, recipes, and songs.

DuBois, Jill. *Israel* (Cultures of the World series). Tarrytown, New York: Marshall Cavendish, 1995. For older readers, offers a brief historical overview and a well-rounded look at modern Israel.

Feirstein, Steve. *Israel . . . in Pictures* (Visual Geography series). Minneapolis: Lerner Publications, 1988. Well-chosen color photographs. A good choice for grades five and up.

Jones, Helen Hinckley. *Enchantment of the World: Israel.* Chicago: Children's Press, 1993. Good text; excellent color photographs.

Lawton, Clive A. *Passport to Israel.* New York: Franklin Watts, 1987. Well-researched text; includes many photos, maps, and graphs.

Shamir, Maxim, and Gabriel Shamir. *The Story of Israel in Stamps.* New York: Sabra Books/Funk & Wagnalls, 1969. Nearly one hundred colorful stamps and accompanying text highlight Israel's first twenty years.

Taitz, Emily, and Sondra Henry. *Israel: A Sacred Land.* Minneapolis: Silver Burdett Press, 1988. Excellent information, clearly presented.

Some of these titles are out of print; they may be available at your local library.

Acknowledgments

Special thanks go to Bluma Zuckerbrot-Finkelstein, Director of Special Projects, Middle Eastern Affairs, for the Anti-Defamation League, for her expert reading of this manuscript. I thank Susan Heller, Director of Middle Eastern Affairs and International Analysis for the Anti-Defamation League, and the Information Department of the Counsel General of Israel in New York for providing helpful information. The interest my daughter, Abigail, and her husband, Alan, evinced in this book meant a great deal to me. So did the support of Margo Lundell and Harriet Rohmer, good friends and good listeners. My mother, Ruth Kusnetzov, was often in my thoughts as I worked on the manuscript. A longtime Hadassah member, her devotion to Israel was an important part of our family life. The suggestions and enthusiasm of my editor, Cindy Kane, and the contributions of the Dial staff were gratefully appreciated. And I am indebted to three people who witnessed history—my friend Margalit Mannor, her mother, Toni Yoel, and Margalit's uncle Avraham—for sharing their remembrances and the story of the doll.

Index

Boldface page numbers refer to illustrations